CW01497701

Deeply Rooted

Exploring God's Word, one day at a time

A Daily Bible Devotional Guide

Written by: Henry C.Ohakah

ISBN: 9798314431009
SPIRIT WIND WORLD IMPACT

As you therefore have received Christ Jesus the Lord, so walk in Him, rooted and built up in Him and established in the faith, as you have been taught, abounding in it with thanksgiving.
 - **Colossians 2:6-7 (NKJV)**

MAY – AUGUST 2025

Dearly beloved in Christ,

It is with great joy that I introduce this quarter's DEEPLY ROOTED DAILY DEVOTIONAL for May to August 2025. Together, we will embark on a meaningful journey through Scripture, drawing wisdom and inspiration from the Word of God. This season's devotional explores various books of the Bible, with a particular focus on *Philippians* and *James*. Philippians, written by the Apostle Paul, offers uplifting insights into faithful and joy-filled living, whilst James challenges us with a call to express our faith through action.

This edition also explores the transformative theme of ENCOUNTERING THE HOLY SPIRIT. We will delve into the Spirit's nature, His transformative work within believers, and His profound impact on the Church. Each day brings an opportunity to reflect on divine truth, uncover practical applications for daily life, and experience growth in both faith and transformation. The reflections will focus on the Spirit's guidance, power, and comfort, inviting us into a Spirit-filled life characterised by worship and purpose.

Altogether, this devotional provides a balanced foundation, equipping us to live out our faith boldly in today's world. It is my prayer that the pages inspire a deeper relationship with the Holy Spirit, shaping every aspect of your walk with Christ. May the insights strengthen your spiritual journey and draw you nearer to God.

In His Grace,

Rev Dr Henry C. Ohakah
Minister, Mountsorrel Baptist Church

MAY 2025

A Bondservant's Heart
THURSDAY, 1 MAY 2025

"Paul And Timothy, Bondservants of Jesus Christ, To All the Saints in Christ Jesus Who Are in Philippi, With the Bishops and Deacons." – Philippians 1:1

The word "Doulos" Paul uses to describe himself - a bondservant - confronts us with the radical nature of discipleship. A bondservant wasn't merely an employee or follower; they were completely devoted to their master, heart, soul, and body. For Paul, being a Doulos of Christ wasn't a badge of limitation but a mark of liberation. He belonged wholly to the One who had set him free. How far are we willing to go in our submission to Jesus? Are we merely admirers, or are we fully yielded servants, living for His glory alone? Reflect today on the areas of your life that still resist His Lordship and ask the Holy Spirit for the courage to live as a true Doulos - utterly devoted, entirely His.

Prayer: Lord, teach me what it means to live as Your bondservant. I surrender every part of my life to You. Lead me to serve You with joy and complete devotion. Amen.

The Gift of Fellowship
FRIDAY, 2 MAY 2025

"I Thank My God Upon Every Remembrance of You, Always in Every Prayer of Mine Making Request for You All with Joy." – Philippians 1:3-4

Fellowship is a gift that transcends human connections. It's the supernatural bond created by the Spirit when believers walk together in faith and purpose. Paul's joy wasn't in fleeting friendships but in the eternal partnership he shared with the Philippians in Christ. His prayers brimmed with gratitude for this divine connection. In a culture marked by isolation, the Church is meant to be a beacon of togetherness. Are you investing in your spiritual community, praying for and walking alongside others in faith? Take time to strengthen these bonds through encouragement, support, or just being present and let the Spirit create joy and unity among His people.

Prayer: Lord, thank You for the gift of fellowship. Help me to cherish and nurture the relationships You've placed in my life, building one another up for Your glory. Amen.

Purpose in the Storm
SATURDAY, 3 MAY 2025

"But I Want You to Know, Brethren, That the Things Which Happened to Me Have Actually Turned Out for The Furtherance of The Gospel." – Philippians 1:12

Paul's imprisonment, though unjust, became a platform for advancing the gospel. What looked like defeat to the world was a victory in the Spirit. Adversity is often the canvas on which God paints His most profound works, using our trials to shine His light into dark places. Are you in a storm today? Don't waste your pain. Surrender it to the Spirit and ask Him to use it for His glory. Just as Paul's chains inspired boldness in others, your faithful endurance can draw people to Jesus, showing them a hope that transcends circumstances.

Prayer: Father, in every trial, help me to see Your hand at work. Strengthen me to trust You and allow my life to be a testimony of Your grace. Amen.

A Life Worthy of the Gospel
SUNDAY, 4 MAY 2025

"Only Let Your Conduct Be Worthy of The Gospel of Christ, So That Whether I Come and See You or Am Absent, I May Hear of Your Affairs, That You Stand Fast in One Spirit, With One Mind Striving Together for The Faith of The Gospel." – Philippians 1:27

Living a life worthy of the gospel is a high calling. It means reflecting the character of Jesus not just in our words but in our actions, unity, and courage. It's about standing firm in faith, striving together as one body, and boldly living out the truth of Christ in a world that desperately needs Him. What does your life say about the gospel? Are your choices, relationships, and priorities aligned with the kingdom of God? The world is watching, and your testimony can either draw people to Christ or drive them away. Let's strive to live in a way that glorifies Him.

Prayer: Lord, let my life be a reflection of Your truth and love. Unite us as one body and empower us to live boldly for Your gospel. Amen.

The Beauty of Christ's Humility
MONDAY, 5 MAY 2025

"Let This Mind Be in You Which Was Also in Christ Jesus." –
Philippians 2:5

The humility of Christ is a paradox - He, being God, emptied Himself, taking on the form of a servant and submitting to death for our sake. It's a humility that doesn't diminish His glory but amplifies His love. This mindset, Paul says, is to be ours. Not self-serving ambition, but selfless surrender. Not seeking recognition but lifting others up. In a world obsessed with pride and self-promotion, Christ's humility challenges us to live differently. Who can you serve today, not for what you gain, but for God's glory? True greatness lies in laying ourselves down for others.

Prayer: Jesus, teach me the beauty of humility. Help me to follow Your example, serving others with grace, love, and a heart that seeks to glorify You alone. Amen.

Shining Brightly
TUESDAY, 6 MAY 2025

"Do All Things Without Complaining and Disputing, That You May Become Blameless and Harmless, Children of God Without Fault in The Midst of a Crooked and Perverse Generation, Among Whom You Shine as Lights in The World." – Philippians 2:14-15

God's children are called to shine like stars against the darkness of a broken world. But this brilliance doesn't come from striving it comes from surrender. Complaining dims our light; gratitude makes it glow. Disputing scatters our witness; unity strengthens it. Are you shining, or has negativity dimmed your reflection of Christ? Today, choose to let go of grumbling and embrace gratitude. Hold fast to the Word of Life and allow His Spirit to radiate through you, making you a beacon of hope and truth.

Prayer: Lord, help me to shine brightly for You in a world filled with darkness. Transform my heart and let my life reflect Your goodness and truth. Amen.

The Timothy Challenge
WEDNESDAY, 7 MAY 2025

"For I Have No One Like-Minded, Who Will Sincerely Care for Your State." – Philippians 2:20

Timothy wasn't extraordinary by the world's standards. Yet, Paul commended him for his genuine care and selfless service. In a world preoccupied with personal gain, Timothy's life challenges us to be people who put others first, serving with the love and compassion of Christ. Who in your life needs a touch of this Christ-like care? Whether through a conversation, a prayer, or an act of kindness, let's commit to being the Timothys of our time - faithful, sincere, and wholly devoted to serving others.

Prayer: Lord, give me a heart like Timothy's, selfless, faithful, and filled with genuine care for others. Help me to reflect Your love in every interaction. Amen.

The Example of Epaphroditus
THURSDAY, 8 MAY 2025

"Yet I Considered It Necessary to Send to You Epaphroditus, My Brother, Fellow Worker, And Fellow Soldier, But Your Messenger and The One Who Ministered to My Need." – Philippians 2:25

Epaphroditus isn't a name that comes up often in sermons, yet his story is one of extraordinary faithfulness. Paul calls him a brother, a fellow worker, and a fellow soldier; titles that speak volumes. Epaphroditus wasn't content with comfortable service; he risked his life for the sake of the gospel. His dedication reminds us that following Christ often requires personal sacrifice. In a culture that prioritises self-preservation and convenience, the example of Epaphroditus confronts us with a challenging question: are we willing to step outside our comfort zones to serve others, even when it costs us? True discipleship isn't about preserving ourselves but pouring ourselves out for the sake of Christ and His Kingdom.

Prayer: Lord, give me the courage to serve selflessly like Epaphroditus. Teach me to prioritise others above myself, trusting in Your provision and strength. Amen.

The Joy of Knowing Christ
FRIDAY, 9 MAY 2025

"But What Things Were Gain to Me, These I Have Counted Loss for Christ. Yet Indeed I Also Count All Things Loss for The Excellence of The Knowledge of Christ Jesus My Lord, For Whom I Have Suffered the Loss of All Things, And Count Them as Rubbish, That I May Gain Christ." – Philippians 3:7-8

Paul's words are deeply convicting. He calls everything - achievements, status, possessions - rubbish when compared to the joy of knowing Christ. It's not that these things don't matter; it's that they pale into insignificance when measured against the surpassing worth of intimacy with Jesus. In a world that equates value with material success, are we willing to place knowing Christ above all else? Does our relationship with Him shape our priorities, or are we chasing after what the world considers gain? True joy and fulfilment are found only in Him.

Prayer: Jesus, help me to value You above all else. Let my heart long for the joy of knowing You deeply and intimately. Amen.

Pressing On Towards the Goal
SATURDAY, 10 MAY 2025

"Not That I Have Already Attained, Or Am Already Perfected; But I Press On, That I May Lay Hold of That for Which Christ Jesus Has Also Laid Hold of Me." – Philippians 3:12

Paul's humility shines through here. He admits he hasn't "arrived," yet his determination to press on is inspiring. Faith is not a static state but a relentless pursuit of Christ, a daily surrender and renewal. The goal isn't perfection in this life but faithfulness to the One who has already laid hold of us. What has Christ taken hold of you for? Are you running your race with perseverance, or have distractions slowed your pace? Let Paul's determination ignite your own resolve to keep pressing on.

Prayer: Lord, help me to press on in my walk with You. Keep me focused on the eternal prize and strengthen me to persevere through every trial. Amen.

Pursuing the Prize
SUNDAY, 11 MAY 2025

"Brethren, I Do Not Count Myself to Have Apprehended; But One Thing I Do, Forgetting Those Things Which Are Behind and Reaching Forward to Those Things Which Are Ahead." – Philippians 3:13

Paul's words echo with urgency and hope. He refuses to let the past whether triumphs or failures hold him back. Instead, he fixes his eyes on what lies ahead, relentlessly pursuing the ultimate prize: Christ Himself. What are you holding onto that might be hindering your race? Guilt, regret, pride, or even nostalgia can anchor us in the past, preventing us from stepping into God's future. Today, choose to release what no longer serves His purpose and press forward in faith.

Prayer: Heavenly Father, help me to release my grip on the past. Teach me to trust You as I reach forward to the future You have planned for me. Amen.

Citizens of Heaven
MONDAY, 12 MAY 2025

"For Our Citizenship Is in Heaven, From Which We Also Eagerly Wait for The Saviour, The Lord Jesus Christ." – Philippians 3:20

Paul reminds us of our true identity: citizens of heaven. This eternal perspective changes everything. When we understand where our ultimate home lies, our priorities shift. Temporal concerns give way to eternal purpose, and our hope rests not in what this world offers but in Christ's return. What does it mean to live as a citizen of heaven today? It means reflecting the values of God's Kingdom - love, justice, humility - in all we do. It means keeping our eyes on the eternal, even as we navigate the challenges of the present.

Prayer: Lord, thank You for the promise of my heavenly citizenship. Help me to live in a way that reflects Your Kingdom and honours You. Amen.

Standing Firm in the Lord
TUESDAY, 13 MAY 2025

"Therefore, My Beloved and Longed-For Brethren, My Joy and Crown, So Stand Fast In The Lord, Beloved." – Philippians 4:1

Paul's love for the Philippians radiates through this verse. He calls them his joy and crown, urging them to remain steadfast in their faith. In today's world, where distractions and opposition abound, standing firm in the Lord demands both courage and conviction. Are we unwavering in our faith, or do we allow the shifting cultural sands to undermine our commitment to Christ? To stand firm doesn't mean to be rigid it means being rooted. Rooted in truth, anchored in grace, and bold enough to reflect the Gospel in both word and deed. Today, ask yourself: Where am I standing? In my own strength, or upon the unshakable foundation of Christ?

Prayer: Father, strengthen my resolve to stand firm in You. May Your truth be my foundation and Your Spirit my guide as I navigate challenges with grace and courage. Amen.

Unity and Reconciliation
WEDNESDAY, 14 MAY 2025

"I Implore Euodia and I Implore Syntyche To Be Of The Same Mind In The Lord." – Philippians 4:2

Even in the early Church, conflict arose, and Paul doesn't shy away from addressing it. His plea for reconciliation between Euodia and Syntyche reminds us that unity is central to the heart of God. Our differences should never outweigh our shared identity in Christ. What relationships in your life need restoration? Unity doesn't mean agreeing on everything but choosing to prioritise love and understanding over division. Today, take a step towards reconciliation. Pray for humility, and let the Spirit lead you in mending what is broken.

Prayer: Lord, bring unity where there is division and peace where there is conflict. Help me to extend grace and seek reconciliation, reflecting Your love in all my relationships. Amen.

Rejoice in the Lord Always
THURSDAY, 15 MAY 2025

"Rejoice In the Lord Always. Again, I Will Say, Rejoice!" – Philippians 4:4

Rejoicing isn't an occasional suggestion it's a command, repeated for emphasis. Paul, writing from a prison cell, demonstrates that joy isn't tethered to our circumstances. It springs from an unshakeable confidence in God's sovereignty and goodness. What's stealing your joy today? Is it fear, disappointment, or unmet expectations? Remember, true joy isn't found in the absence of trouble but in the presence of Christ. Choose to rejoice not in what's temporary, but in the eternal.

Prayer: Jesus, let my joy be rooted in You, not my circumstances. Teach me to rejoice always, trusting in Your unchanging goodness and grace. Amen.

The Power of Gentleness
FRIDAY, 16 MAY 2025

"Let Your Gentleness Be Known to All Men. The Lord Is at Hand." – Philippians 4:5

Gentleness is often misunderstood as weakness, but in the Kingdom of God, it's a profound strength. It disarms hostility, breaks down barriers, and reflects the heart of Jesus. In a world that celebrates aggression and dominance, choosing gentleness is a radical act of faith. How do you respond to conflict or criticism? Gentleness doesn't mean avoiding truth but delivering it with humility and grace. Be mindful today of your words and actions, allowing the Spirit to shape them into a reflection of Christ's love.

Prayer: Lord, cultivate in me a gentle spirit that reflects Your love. Help me to respond with kindness, even in difficult situations, and to be a witness of Your grace. Amen.

Prayer that Brings Peace
SATURDAY, 17 MAY 2025

"Be Anxious for Nothing, But in Everything by Prayer and Supplication, With Thanksgiving, Let Your Requests Be Made Known to God." – Philippians 4:6

Paul doesn't say we won't face anxiety; he invites us to respond to it differently. Instead of allowing worry to consume us, we're called to bring every concern to God in prayer. But notice the qualifier: with thanksgiving. Gratitude shifts our focus from the size of our problem to the greatness of our God. When was the last time you turned your worries into prayers? Let today be a day of surrender. Lay your burdens at His feet, and trust that His peace beyond understanding will guard your heart and mind.

Prayer: Father, thank You for inviting me to bring my burdens to You. Replace my anxiety with Your peace and remind me of Your constant presence and care. Amen.

The Peace of God
SUNDAY, 18 MAY 2025

"And The Peace of God, Which Surpasses All Understanding, Will Guard Your Hearts and Minds Through Christ Jesus." – Philippians 4:7

Paul's words offer more than a sentiment; they declare a reality rooted in Christ. This peace isn't passive or circumstantial it is active and eternal. It shields our hearts and minds in ways the world cannot comprehend, even when chaos surrounds us. Consider the state of our world today: conflicts rage from Israel to Ukraine, and communities in Sudan, Myanmar, and Yemen are torn apart by violence. Yet, amidst such brokenness, Paul assures us that God's peace remains steadfast. This peace reminds us that our hope is not anchored in earthly resolutions but in the unshakable presence of Christ. Are you seeking this peace in your own life? It requires surrender - a relinquishing of worry and control into the hands of the One who holds all things together. Today, trust Him to guard your heart and mind, allowing His peace to steady you no matter the storm.

Prayer: Lord, thank You for a peace that surpasses understanding. Guard my heart and mind in Christ and help me reflect this peace in a world desperate for hope. Amen.

Meditate on These Things
MONDAY, 19 MAY 2025

"Finally, Brethren, Whatever Things Are True, Whatever Things Are Noble, Whatever Things Are Just, Whatever Things Are Pure, Whatever Things Are Lovely, Whatever Things Are of Good Report, If There Is Any Virtue and If There Is Anything Praiseworthy—Meditate on These Things." – Philippians 4:8

Your thoughts are the compass of your soul, guiding your attitudes and actions. Paul's instruction here is both a challenge and a lifeline in a world saturated with negativity. To meditate on what is true and noble requires discipline and intentionality, especially when we're bombarded with messages that glorify fear, division, or despair. What fills your mind today? Are your thoughts aligned with God's truth, or are they weighed down by the distractions of this world? Take time to recalibrate. Invite the Holy Spirit to help you dwell on what is pure and praiseworthy, allowing your thought life to reflect His glory.

Prayer: Father, renew my mind. Help me to meditate on what honours You and transforms my heart. May my thoughts bring me closer to You and inspire my actions. Amen.

Contentment in All Circumstances
TUESDAY, 20 MAY 2025

"I Know How to Be Abased, And I Know How to Abound. Everywhere And in All Things, I Have Learned Both to Be Full and To Be Hungry, Both To Abound And To Suffer Need." – Philippians 4:12

Paul's contentment wasn't circumstantial it was deeply rooted in Christ. Whether in scarcity or abundance, he discovered the secret of a heart satisfied not by possessions, but by presence: the presence of Jesus. What about you? Are you chasing after the world's "more," or are you resting in the sufficiency of Christ? True contentment is a discipline cultivated in both prosperity and want. It's choosing gratitude over grumbling, trust over striving. Today, invite Jesus to teach you the joy of being content in Him alone.

Prayer: Lord, teach me the secret of true contentment. Let me find satisfaction not in possessions but in Your presence, trusting You in all circumstances. Amen.

Joy in Trials
WEDNESDAY, 21 MAY 2025

"My Brethren, Count It All Joy When You Fall into Various Trials, Knowing That the Testing of Your Faith Produces Patience." – James 1:2-3

Joy in trials feels counterintuitive, but it's a mark of mature faith. Trials refine us, stripping away what is temporary and revealing what is eternal. They teach us patience and deepen our trust in God. Are you facing a trial today? Don't waste it. Choose to see it as an opportunity for growth, a chance to see God's power at work in your life. Joy isn't the absence of struggle it is the presence of hope, knowing that your trials are producing something far greater than they appear.

Prayer: Lord, thank You for refining me through trials. Help me to see challenges as opportunities for growth and fill me with joy rooted in Your promises. Amen.

Seeking Divine Wisdom
THURSDAY, 22 MAY 2025

"If Any of You Lacks Wisdom, Let Him Ask of God, Who Gives to All Liberally and Without Reproach, And It Will Be Given to Him." – James 1:5

God's wisdom is a gift, not a reward for the deserving. It is given freely to those humble enough to ask. Whether in times of confusion, failure, or decision-making, His wisdom illuminates the path forward. What decision or challenge are you wrestling with today? Have you asked God for His wisdom, or are you relying on your own understanding? Bring your concerns to Him, trusting that He delights in guiding His children. His wisdom not only equips but also transforms, leading you to a life aligned with His will.

Prayer: Father, I surrender my understanding and seek Your wisdom. Illuminate my path and guide me in every decision I face. Amen.

Faith in Action
FRIDAY, 23 MAY 2025

"But Be Doers of The Word, And Not Hearers Only, Deceiving Yourselves." – James 1:22

Faith that doesn't act isn't faith at all. It's easy to nod in agreement with God's Word, but true discipleship requires obedience. When we live out our faith whether through kindness, forgiveness, or justice we become vessels of His love and truth. How is your faith being expressed today? Are you merely hearing the Word, or are you putting it into action? Let this be a day of living faith, where your deeds reflect your devotion to Christ.

Prayer: Lord, let my faith be more than words. Empower me to live out Your truth in tangible ways, bringing glory to Your name. Amen.

Taming the Tongue
SATURDAY, 24 MAY 2025

"If Anyone Among You Thinks He Is Religious, And Does Not Bridle His Tongue But Deceives His Own Heart, This One's Religion Is Useless." – James 1:26

The tongue, though small, holds immense power. It can edify or destroy, inspire or wound. James compels us to confront the connection between our faith and our speech, reminding us that our words are not insignificant, they have the power to shape realities. As I wrote in my book, *Speak To Your Future: You Are The Prophet Of Your Own Life,* "words are living things." They carry the weight of life and influence, impacting both the speaker and the listener. When challenges arise, we often allow words of frustration or defeat to slip out, unwittingly magnifying the difficulty. Yet God, in His grace, invites us to transform our speech, replacing negativity with declarations grounded in His promises. This transformation is not instant it requires intentionality and faith. But as we choose to speak life, our mindset and circumstances shift. Controlling the tongue isn't merely about holding back harsh words. It's about choosing to reflect Christ's love, truth, and hope in all we say. True faith is revealed when our words uplift and direct others toward God's grace. Your words carry the power to build or break. In moments of frustration, uncertainty, or joy, remember: "words are living things." Speak truth, life, and grace in every situation, trusting God to work through your speech to bring hope and transformation.

Prayer: Father, teach me to bridle my tongue and speak words that build others up. May my words reflect Your love and grace, bringing encouragement and hope to those around me. Amen.

Avoiding Partiality
SUNDAY, 25 MAY 2025

"My Brethren, Do Not Hold the Faith of Our Lord Jesus Christ, The Lord of Glory, With Partiality." – James 2:1

Faith in Christ calls us to live above the prejudice and favouritism that so often define human interactions. Jesus' encounter with the Samaritan woman is a profound example of this. He broke every social boundary - ethnicity, gender, and reputation - choosing instead to see her as a person of value, worthy of truth and grace. How often do we judge people based on appearances, status, or background? This passage challenges us to see others through God's eyes, extending the same love and respect to all. Today, examine your heart. Are there areas where partiality has crept in? Let the Holy Spirit transform your perspective.

Prayer: Lord, cleanse my heart of all prejudice. Teach me to see others as You see them and help me to reflect Your love and grace to everyone I meet. Amen.

Living Faith
MONDAY, 26 MAY 2025

"Thus, Also Faith by Itself, If It Does Not Have Works, Is Dead." – James 2:17

Faith is not passive it is active and alive, revealed through the way we live. James emphasises this truth: genuine faith is evidenced by our actions. Whether serving through a ministry like the Food Project or helping a neighbour in need, our deeds reflect the reality of Christ at work within us. Where is your faith leading you today? Consider how you can put your beliefs into action. Faith without works is stagnant, but faith that serves becomes a light that draws others to Jesus.

Prayer: Lord, let my faith be vibrant and active. Show me opportunities to serve others and reflect Your love in everything I do. Amen.

Controlling the Tongue
TUESDAY, 27 MAY 2025

"Even So the Tongue Is a Little Member and Boasts Great Things. See How Great a Forest a Little Fire Kindles!" – James 3:5

The tongue holds incredible power. It can build up or tear down, heal or wound. James warns us that careless words can ignite fires of destruction, while Spirit-led speech brings life and encouragement. What words are you speaking today? Take a moment to reflect before you speak. Are your words a reflection of God's truth, or do they sow discord and hurt? Ask the Holy Spirit to help you bridle your tongue and speak life into every situation.

Prayer: Father, let my words reflect Your love and truth. Help me to speak with wisdom and kindness, building up rather than tearing down. Amen.

Drawing Near to God
WEDNESDAY, 28 MAY 2025

"Draw Near to God and He Will Draw Near to You. Cleanse Your Hands, You Sinners; And Purify Your Hearts, You Double-Minded." – James 4:8

God's invitation is clear: come closer. But drawing near to Him requires us to cleanse our hands and purify our hearts, removing anything that hinders our relationship with Him. This is a call to intentionality, to prioritise His presence above all else. Are you making space for God in your life? Amid the busyness and distractions, take time today to seek Him in prayer, worship, and His Word. The promise is simple yet profound: as we draw near to Him, He draws near to us.

Prayer: Lord, I long to be closer to You. Help me to purify my heart, remove distractions, and prioritise time in Your presence. Amen.

Submitting to God
THURSDAY, 29 MAY 2025

"Therefore, Submit to God. Resist The Devil and He Will Flee from You." – James 4:7

Submission to God is the first step in standing against the enemy. When we yield our will to His, we align ourselves with His power and protection. Resisting the devil isn't a solo effort it is a Spirit-empowered act of faith. What areas of your life need surrender today? Submission isn't weakness; it's recognising God's strength in our lives. Trust Him, resist the enemy, and watch how He works on your behalf.

Prayer: Father, I submit every area of my life to You. Strengthen me to resist the enemy and stand firm in Your power. Amen.

Humility and Grace
FRIDAY, 30 MAY 2025

"But He Gives More Grace. Therefore, He Says: 'God Resists the Proud, But Gives Grace to The Humble.'" – James 4:6

Grace flows to the humble, but pride creates resistance between us and God. Humility isn't thinking less of ourselves but recognising our dependence on Him. It's the foundation of a surrendered life that reflects Christ. Are you clinging to pride in any area of your life? Ask God to help you let go and embrace humility, opening your heart to the fullness of His grace. True strength comes when we acknowledge our need for Him.

Prayer: Lord, I surrender my pride and open my heart to Your grace. Teach me to walk humbly before You and to serve others selflessly. Amen.

The Gift of Prayer
SATURDAY, 31 MAY 2025

"The Effective, Fervent Prayer of a Righteous Man Avails Much."
– James 5:16

Prayer is one of the most powerful tools God has given us. Through it, we communicate with Him, align our hearts to His will, and see His hand move in our lives and the lives of others. As John Wesley once said, *"God Does Nothing but By Prayer, And Everything with It."* How is your prayer life? Are you fervent and expectant, or has it become routine? Today, recommit to a life of prayer, trusting that God hears and answers according to His perfect will.

Prayer: Heavenly Father, thank You for the gift of prayer. Teach me to pray fervently and faithfully, seeking Your presence and aligning my heart with Yours. Amen.

JUNE 2025

Living by Faith
SUNDAY, 1 JUNE 2025

"Now Faith Is Confidence in What We Hope for And Assurance About What We Do Not See." – Hebrews 11:1

Faith is the foundation upon which our relationship with God is built. It's not merely a fleeting feeling or blind optimism; it is a deliberate and resolute trust in His promises, even when the path ahead is clouded by uncertainty. Faith calls us to lean not on what we can see or control but on the One who knows the end from the beginning. Reflecting on my own journey of moving to the UK, I experienced firsthand how faith guides us through uncharted waters. Every challenge - navigating new systems, adapting to cultural norms, and building relationships - was an opportunity to trust that God was orchestrating something greater. He didn't reveal the whole picture at once, but with every step of obedience, His faithfulness became evident. Faith required action, a willingness to step forward even when the outcome was unclear. What situation in your life is calling for faith today? It may feel daunting but remember that faith activates God's promises. It opens the door for His power to work in ways beyond what you can imagine. Let your confidence be not in what you see but in the One who is working all things for your good.

Prayer: Heavenly Father, help me to live by faith, not by sight. Strengthen my trust in Your promises, and guide me to walk boldly, knowing that You are with me every step of the way. Amen.

The Power of Love
MONDAY, 2 JUNE 2025

"And Now These Three Remain: Faith, Hope and Love. But The Greatest of These Is Love." – 1 Corinthians 13:13

Love is not just a virtue; it is the essence of God Himself. It is through love that the world glimpses His character. Yet, love is not always easy. It requires patience when we're rushed, kindness when we feel slighted, and selflessness in a culture that often glorifies personal gain. Think about someone in your life who might need to experience Christ's love through you. Perhaps it's a colleague who feels overlooked, a family member who's hurt you, or even a stranger who crosses your path today. Love is powerful because it reflects God's heart, it heals, restores, and transforms. Love doesn't always come naturally, but it becomes possible when we stay connected to the source. As we abide in Christ, His love flows through us, allowing us to love even when it's difficult. Let today be marked by choices to love intentionally, sacrificially, and unconditionally.

Prayer: Lord, fill my heart with Your love so that I can reflect it to those around me. Teach me to love others as You have loved me, with patience, kindness, and grace. Amen.

Forgiveness and Grace
TUESDAY, 3 JUNE 2025

"Be Kind and Compassionate To One Another, Forgiving Each Other, Just as In Christ God Forgave You." – Ephesians 4:32

Forgiveness is one of the hardest acts of faith, yet one of the most liberating. When we choose to forgive, we echo the grace we've received through Christ. It's not about denying the hurt or excusing the offence; it's about letting go of the bitterness that binds our hearts. The story of Corrie ten Boom exemplifies the divine strength required for forgiveness. Standing face-to-face with a former concentration camp guard, she had every reason to refuse. But as she extended her hand in faith, God's grace filled the gap between her human inability and His supernatural love. Is there someone you need to forgive? Perhaps you've been carrying resentment for too long. Forgiveness doesn't change the past, but it does change your heart, making room for healing and peace. Trust that God will meet you in the process, just as He did with Corrie.

Prayer: Heavenly Father, thank You for forgiving me through Christ. Teach me to extend that same forgiveness to others, even when it's difficult. Free me from bitterness and fill my heart with Your grace. Amen.

The Fruit of the Spirit
WEDNESDAY, 4 JUNE 2025

"But The Fruit of The Spirit Is Love, Joy, Peace, Forbearance, Kindness, Goodness, Faithfulness, Gentleness and Self-Control. Against Such Things There Is No Law." – Galatians 5:22-23

The fruit of the Spirit is evidence of a life that abides in Christ. These qualities are not achieved through effort alone but are cultivated as we surrender to the Holy Spirit's work within us. Which of these do you find most challenging? Perhaps patience feels impossible when life's demands are relentless, or self-control falters in moments of frustration. The good news is that God doesn't ask us to cultivate the fruit on our own. He invites us to remain in Him, and as we do, His Spirit works in us to produce a harvest that glorifies Him. Take time today to reflect on how these qualities are showing up in your life. Ask the Holy Spirit to strengthen the areas where you are weak and to help you shine as a reflection of Christ's character.

Prayer: Lord, let Your Spirit transform me. Cultivate in me the fruit that reflects Your love and draws others to You. May my life bear witness to Your power and grace. Amen.

The Importance of Humility
THURSDAY, 5 JUNE 2025

"Do Nothing Out of Selfish Ambition or Vain Conceit. Rather, In Humility Value Others Above Yourselves." – Philippians 2:3

True humility is not thinking less of yourself but thinking of yourself less. It is recognising that every gift, talent, and opportunity comes from God and using them to serve others. Humility challenges us to step out of the spotlight and lift others up instead. In a world that often equates humility with weakness, God reminds us that it is the path to greatness in His Kingdom. Jesus, the King of kings, humbled Himself to wash the feet of His disciples, showing us what servant leadership looks like. How can you practise humility today? Whether by listening more attentively, offering encouragement, or sacrificing your own convenience for someone else's benefit, let your actions reflect the heart of Christ.

Prayer: Father, teach me to walk in humility. Help me to value others above myself and to serve with a heart of love and grace. Let my life point to You in all that I do. Amen.

Being a Light in the World
FRIDAY, 6 JUNE 2025

"In The Same Way, Let Your Light Shine Before Others, That They May See Your Good Deeds and Glorify Your Father in Heaven." – Matthew 5:16

Jesus calls us to live in a way that radiates His love and truth to a world often shrouded in darkness. This light isn't merely about public displays of goodness but an authentic reflection of Christ's transformative power within us. What does your light look like today? It doesn't need to be grandiose. A simple act of kindness, a word of encouragement, or standing firm in truth when others falter can illuminate Christ's presence to those around you. Your life might be the only Gospel someone ever reads. Let your words and actions be windows through which others glimpse God's love. In a world searching for hope, choose to shine with the humility, joy, and grace that point directly to Him.

Prayer: Lord, help me to live as a reflection of Your light. Let my words and actions glorify You and draw others closer to Your love. Amen.

Trusting in God's Plan
SATURDAY, 7 JUNE 2025

"Trust In the Lord with All Your Heart and Lean Not on Your Own Understanding; In All Your Ways Submit to Him, And He Will Make Your Paths Straight." – Proverbs 3:5-6

Trusting God's plan often requires surrendering our desire for control. It demands faith, particularly when His ways seem unclear or counter to our own understanding. Think of a time when your plans unravelled, leaving you unsure of what to do next. How did God guide you through? His wisdom far exceeds ours, and though the road may be winding, His paths are always good and lead to His purpose. Today, lay your plans and uncertainties at His feet. Trust that His guidance will align you with His perfect will even when the outcome isn't immediately visible.

Prayer: Father, teach me to trust You fully. Strengthen my faith and grant me the courage to surrender my plans to Your perfect wisdom. Amen.

The Power of God's Word
SUNDAY, 8 JUNE 2025

"For The Word of God Is Alive and Active. Sharper Than Any Double-Edged Sword, It Penetrates Even to Dividing Soul and Spirit, Joints and Marrow; It Judges the Thoughts and Attitudes of The Heart." – Hebrews 4:12

God's Word is not a static text; it's a living, breathing force that transforms hearts and minds. Scripture has the unique power to reveal truths about us, convicting us where we need to grow and guiding us in righteousness. When was the last time you allowed the Word to speak directly into your life? Make time today to meditate on Scripture, listening for the Spirit's voice. His Word will not only strengthen your faith but also equip you to face life's challenges with courage and clarity.

Prayer: Lord, thank You for the power of Your Word. Help me to approach it with an open heart, ready to be transformed by Your truth. Amen.

The Importance of Community
MONDAY, 9 JUNE 2025

"And Let Us Consider How We May Spur One Another On Toward Love and Good Deeds, Not Giving Up Meeting Together, As Some Are in The Habit of Doing, But Encouraging One Another – And All the More as You See the Day Approaching." – Hebrews 10:24-25

We were never meant to walk this faith journey alone. Community is a gift from God that provides encouragement, accountability, and shared spiritual growth. It's within these gatherings that we find strength to persevere and opportunities to practise love and service. Are you investing in your spiritual community? Whether through attending church, participating in a small group, or simply reaching out to a fellow believer, take intentional steps to build connections that uplift and inspire.

Prayer: Heavenly Father, thank You for the gift of community. Help me to be an encourager and to spur others on towards love and good deeds. Amen.

Living with Integrity
TUESDAY, 10 JUNE 2025

"Whoever Walks in Integrity Walks Securely, But Whoever Takes Crooked Paths Will Be Found Out." – Proverbs 10:9

Integrity is living with consistency between our words and actions. It's choosing honesty over deceit, even when no one is watching. A life of integrity honours God and builds trust with others. Reflect on your recent choices and interactions. Are they marked by truthfulness and fairness? Ask the Holy Spirit to strengthen you where integrity has wavered, and walk confidently, knowing that nothing hidden is concealed from God.

Prayer: Lord, guide my steps in truth and integrity. Help me to honour You in all areas of my life and to be a witness of Your righteousness. Amen.

The Gift of Generosity
WEDNESDAY, 11 JUNE 2025

"Each Of You Should Give What You Have Decided in Your Heart to Give, Not Reluctantly or Under Compulsion, For God Loves a Cheerful Giver." – 2 Corinthians 9:7

True generosity stems from the heart, shaped not by obligation but by joy. It is a beautiful reflection of God's open-handed love, offering us the privilege of mirroring His character. Generosity extends far beyond material possessions; it embraces time, energy, and even the smallest acts of kindness that leave a lasting impact on others. When we give freely and cheerfully, something transformative happens. The act of giving not only blesses those around us but also reshapes our own hearts, drawing us closer to God's loving nature. It's not about the size of the gift, but the spirit with which it is given - a heart aligned with gratitude and compassion. Who in your life could benefit from an act of generosity today? Perhaps a struggling friend, a colleague in need of encouragement, or a cause that resonates with your heart. Whether through material resources, a kind word, or your time, let your actions reflect God's boundless love and inspire hope in others.

Prayer: Loving Father, cultivate within me a heart of generosity. Let my giving flow freely and joyfully, rooted in gratitude for all that You have provided. May my actions bring blessing to others and glorify Your name. Amen.

Walking in Wisdom
THURSDAY, 12 JUNE 2025

"The Fear of The Lord Is the Beginning of Wisdom, And Knowledge of The Holy One Is Understanding." – Proverbs 9:10

Wisdom begins with reverence for God, recognising His sovereignty and seeking His guidance above all else. It's not about knowing every answer but trusting that God directs our steps when we seek Him first. What decisions are you facing today? Bring them before God, asking for His wisdom. Let His Word and Spirit guide you to paths that honour Him and bring peace.

Prayer: Lord, grant me Your wisdom as I navigate life's challenges. Help me to seek Your understanding above my own. Amen.

Strength in Weakness
FRIDAY, 13 JUNE 2025

"But He Said to Me, 'My Grace Is Sufficient for You, For My Power Is Made Perfect in Weakness.' Therefore I Will Boast All The More Gladly About My Weaknesses, So That Christ's Power May Rest On Me." – 2 Corinthians 12:9

Our weaknesses are opportunities for God's strength to shine through us. Instead of hiding or resenting our shortcomings, we can embrace them, trusting that His grace is sufficient to carry us through. When you feel inadequate or overwhelmed today, lean into God's grace. His power is not hindered by your weakness it is amplified by it.

Prayer: Lord, thank You for meeting me in my weaknesses. Let Your strength be my refuge and Your grace my confidence. Amen.

The Joy of the Lord
SATURDAY, 14 JUNE 2025

"The Joy of The Lord Is Your Strength." — Nehemiah 8:10

True joy is not tied to fleeting emotions or favourable circumstances; it is rooted in the unchanging character of God. This joy, anchored in His presence, becomes a wellspring of strength when we face life's challenges. Think about the times when joy has sustained you not the shallow happiness that depends on external success, but the deep, abiding joy that comes from knowing you belong to Him. Worship is a powerful way to access this joy. When we praise God, even in trials, our perspective shifts from the weight of our problems to the greatness of His promises. How can you let the joy of the Lord strengthen you today? Perhaps through moments of gratitude, singing a song of praise, or meditating on His faithfulness. Let His joy fill your heart and renew your spirit.

Prayer: Lord, let Your joy be my foundation and strength. Help me to focus on You in every season, allowing Your presence to refresh and sustain me. Amen.

Loving Your Neighbour
SUNDAY, 15 JUNE 2025

"Love Your Neighbour as Yourself." – Matthew 22:39

Loving your neighbour is not just an ideal; it's a command that reflects the very heart of God. This love is not reserved for those who are easy to love. It extends to the difficult, the hurting, and even the ones who may have wronged us. Loving others as yourself means extending the same kindness, understanding, and care that you would hope to receive. Is there someone in your life who could benefit from this love today? It may be through a listening ear, a thoughtful gesture, or a choice to forgive. These actions may seem small, but they carry eternal significance, planting seeds of grace and hope in the hearts of those around you.

Prayer: Lord, teach me to love selflessly and generously. May my actions be a reflection of Your compassion, bringing encouragement to those around me and drawing them closer to You. Amen.

Patience and Perseverance
MONDAY, 16 JUNE 2025

"Let Perseverance Finish Its Work So That You May Be Mature and Complete, Not Lacking Anything." – James 1:4

Perseverance is the holy tension of trusting God in the waiting, knowing that every trial holds purpose. It shapes us, chiselling away impatience, pride, and fear, creating something beautiful in their place: spiritual maturity. Growth doesn't happen overnight it is a process. But take heart, for the One who began the work in you is faithful to finish it. Think of challenges as spiritual training grounds. They may test your patience, but they also build your faith. When you're tempted to throw in the towel, ask God for the strength to endure. Trust that through every trial, He is refining you for a deeper purpose.

Prayer: Father, grant me the patience to endure trials with faith. Help me to trust that You are using every challenge to shape me into the person You've called me to be. Amen.

Hope in God
TUESDAY, 17 JUNE 2025

"Why, My Soul, Are You Downcast? Why So Disturbed Within Me? Put Your Hope in God, For I Will Yet Praise Him, My Saviour and My God." – Psalm 42:11

There are seasons when discouragement weighs heavy, and the path ahead feels uncertain. Yet, even in those moments, hope in God becomes the anchor of our souls. His promises are steady, and His love unshakeable. Take time to reflect today: where have you seen God's faithfulness before? Perhaps in answered prayers, unexpected provision, or the peace that carried you through storms. Let those memories remind your soul of His unchanging goodness. Praise Him not for the absence of struggle, but for His presence in the midst of it.

Prayer: Lord, restore my hope when I feel overwhelmed. Remind me of Your faithfulness and help me to trust in You through every season. Amen.

Serving with a Willing Heart
WEDNESDAY, 18 JUNE 2025

"Serve Wholeheartedly, As If You Were Serving the Lord, Not People." – Ephesians 6:7

True service is an act of worship. It flows not from obligation but from a heart that seeks to glorify God. Serving with joy and willingness transforms even the simplest tasks into profound acts of love. Reflecting on my own journey, I recall the joy of volunteering at the food bank in Sheffield. What began as a practical task became a powerful lesson in being present - "loitering with intent," as the Methodists say. It was in those moments of intentional service that I witnessed the beauty of small acts of kindness creating lasting impact. What opportunities do you have to serve today? Whether at home, work, or in your community, let every action be done as unto the Lord, knowing that even the unseen acts of love bring glory to Him.

Prayer: Lord, teach me to serve with a joyful and willing heart. May my actions reflect Your love and draw others closer to You. Amen.

God's Unfailing Love
THURSDAY, 19 JUNE 2025

"The Lord Is Compassionate and Gracious, Slow to Anger, Abounding in Love." – Psalm 103:8

God's love is not conditional, nor is it fleeting. It is steadfast, unwavering, and abundant. He meets us with compassion, even in our failures, and His grace covers us in ways we can't fully comprehend. Take a moment today to meditate on His love. Think about the ways He has shown up in your life through answered prayers, unexpected blessings, or the quiet assurance of His presence. As you reflect, consider how you might extend that same love to those around you, embodying His grace and compassion.

Prayer: Lord, thank You for loving me unconditionally. Help me to be a vessel of Your love, showing grace and kindness to others as You have shown to me. Amen.

Embracing God's Peace
FRIDAY, 20 JUNE 2025

"Peace I Leave With You; My Peace I Give You. I Do Not Give to You as The World Gives. Do Not Let Your Hearts Be Troubled and Do Not Be Afraid." – John 14:27

God's peace is unlike anything the world offers. It's not fleeting or dependent on circumstances it is a deep-seated assurance that He is in control, even when life feels chaotic. When anxiety or worry threatens to overtake you, take a moment to pause. Surrender your burdens to God in prayer and ask Him to fill you with His peace. Let His presence quiet your fears and remind you that His power is greater than any challenge you face.

Prayer: Lord, thank You for the gift of Your peace. Help me to trust in Your promises and rest in the knowledge that You are with me. Amen.

Trusting God's Guidance
SATURDAY, 21 JUNE 2025

"Whether You Turn to The Right or To the Left, Your Ears Will Hear a Voice Behind You, Saying, 'This Is the Way; Walk in It.'" – Isaiah 30:21

God is always speaking through His Word, through circumstances, and through His Spirit within us. The challenge lies in quieting the noise of life to hear His voice clearly. What decisions or uncertainties are you facing today? Take intentional time to unplug from distractions and seek His guidance. Trust that He is faithful to lead you, even when the way forward is unclear. His Spirit doesn't just show the path He walks it with you.

Prayer: Holy Spirit, guide me in Your truth. Help me to hear Your voice above the noise and to trust Your leading in every area of my life. Amen.

Bearing Fruit
SUNDAY, 22 JUNE 2025

"The Fruit of The Righteous Is a Tree of Life, And the One Who Is Wise Saves Lives." – Proverbs 11:30

"But The Fruit of The Spirit Is Love, Joy, Peace, Forbearance, Kindness, Goodness, Faithfulness, Gentleness, And Self-Control." – Galatians 5:22-23

A life rooted in Christ naturally bears fruit that nourishes and blesses others. The Spirit's work in us is evident through our attitudes and actions, reflecting His love and transforming lives. What fruit is the Spirit producing in your life? Are there areas where you struggle to exhibit love, patience, or kindness? Ask Him to strengthen you, leaning on His power to respond with grace even in challenging circumstances.

Prayer: Lord, let my life be a reflection of Your Spirit's work. Help me to bear fruit that glorifies You and draws others closer to Your love. Amen.

Empowered for Mission
MONDAY, 23 JUNE 2025

"'Not By Might nor By Power, But by My Spirit,' Says the Lord Almighty." – Zechariah 4:6

"But You Will Receive Power When the Holy Spirit Comes on You; And You Will Be My Witnesses in Jerusalem, And in All Judea and Samaria, And to The Ends of The Earth." – Acts 1:8

Sharing the Gospel isn't about relying on our own abilities. It is the Holy Spirit that equips, emboldens, and empowers us to live as witnesses for Christ. This power isn't reserved for a select few; it is the inheritance of every believer. Whether it's standing up for truth in a conversation, serving with humility, or extending hope to someone in despair, the Spirit provides everything we need to reflect His glory. Think about the areas where God may be calling you to step out in boldness. Is there someone in your circle who needs encouragement, prayer, or a listening ear? Trust that the Holy Spirit will give you the right words and the courage to share His love. Be intentional today about being a witness for Christ. Whether through your testimony, acts of service, or kindness, let others see His light through you.

Prayer: Spirit of God, fill me with boldness and power to be Your witness. Help me reflect Your truth and love in every interaction. Amen.

Renewed Strength
TUESDAY, 24 JUNE 2025

"But Those Who Hope in The Lord Will Renew Their Strength. They Will Soar on Wings Like Eagles; They Will Run and Not Grow Weary, They Will Walk and Not Be Faint." – Isaiah 40:31

"Therefore We Do Not Lose Heart. Though Outwardly We Are Wasting Away, Yet Inwardly We Are Being Renewed Day by Day." – 2 Corinthians 4:16

In a world that glorifies busyness and self-reliance, it's easy to feel depleted. But God never intended for us to operate on empty. His promise is clear: when we place our hope in Him, He renews our strength daily. This renewal isn't just physical it is spiritual and emotional, enabling us to persevere in faith even when the road feels long. Where do you need renewed strength today? Pause and invite the Holy Spirit to refresh you. Let go of the pressure to do it all on your own and rest in the assurance that His power is sufficient. Take a moment today to step away from busyness. Pray and meditate on God's promises, allowing His presence to recharge your heart and mind.

Prayer: Holy Spirit, renew my strength today. Fill me with Your peace and energy so I can live fully for You, even in challenging seasons. Amen.

Walking in Unity
WEDNESDAY, 25 JUNE 2025

"How Good and Pleasant It Is When God's People Live Together in Unity!" – Psalm 133:1

"Make Every Effort to Keep the Unity of The Spirit Through the Bond of Peace." – Ephesians 4:3

Unity within the body of Christ is a powerful testimony to the world. It reflects the reconciliation made possible by the Spirit. Yet, unity doesn't mean uniformity. It means embracing diversity with grace and seeking common ground in Christ. Do you have unresolved tension or conflict with someone? Today is an opportunity to take a step towards healing. Unity requires humility, forgiveness, and the willingness to prioritise relationships over personal differences. Reach out to someone you may be in conflict with and ask the Holy Spirit to guide the conversation. Even a small gesture of reconciliation can bring peace and healing.

Prayer: Lord, help me to walk in unity with others. Break down barriers of pride and misunderstanding, and let Your Spirit bring peace and harmony to our relationships. Amen.

Standing Firm in Faith
THURSDAY, 26 JUNE 2025

"The Sovereign Lord Is My Strength; He Makes My Feet Like the Feet of a Deer, He Enables Me to Tread on The Heights." – Habakkuk 3:19

"Be On Your Guard; Stand Firm in The Faith; Be Courageous; Be Strong." – 1 Corinthians 16:13

Challenges to our faith are inevitable, whether they come as opposition, temptation, or doubt. Yet the Holy Spirit strengthens us to stand firm and courageous, even when the world pushes against us. Faith isn't about avoiding difficulty; it's about trusting God through it. Where have you felt pressure to compromise your faith? Remember, the Spirit equips you to remain steadfast. Lean on Scripture and seek encouragement from fellow believers to fortify your heart. Reflect on areas where you've struggled to stand firm in faith. Pray for wisdom, courage, and strength to remain unwavering.

Prayer: Holy Spirit, strengthen my faith and give me courage to stand firm in Your truth, no matter what challenges I face. Amen.

A Life of Worship
FRIDAY, 27 JUNE 2025

"Let Everything That Has Breathe Praise the Lord. Praise The Lord." – Psalm 150:6

"God Is Spirit, And His Worshippers Must Worship in The Spirit and In Truth." – John 4:24

Worship isn't confined to Sunday mornings or set apart for times of song. It's a lifestyle that honours God in every moment. When we live in the Spirit, even the simplest tasks become acts of worship, as we acknowledge His presence and give Him glory. How can you worship God in your daily routines? Whether it's through a thankful heart, excellence in your work, or intentional praise, let your life reflect a heart devoted to Him. Take time to express worship to God in your routine today. It could be through gratitude, prayer, or simply pausing to acknowledge His presence.

Prayer: Lord, let my life be an offering of worship to You. Help me to honour You in all I do and to keep my heart centred on Your Spirit. Amen.

Being Transformed
SATURDAY, 28 JUNE 2025

"I Will Give You a New Heart and Put a New Spirit in You; I Will Remove from You Your Heart of Stone and Give You a Heart of Flesh." – Ezekiel 36:26

"And We All, Who with Unveiled Faces Contemplate the Lord's Glory, Are Being Transformed into His Image with Ever-Increasing Glory, Which Comes from The Lord, Who Is the Spirit." – 2 Corinthians 3:18

Transformation is the Spirit's masterpiece. It's not about superficial changes but deep renewal - reshaping our hearts, attitudes, and desires to reflect Christ. This process, though often uncomfortable, is one of the most beautiful expressions of God's grace in our lives. Imagine a potter at work moulding, smoothing, and refining, that's what the Holy Spirit does in us. The habits we once clung to lose their grip, and Christlike character takes their place. But transformation requires surrender. It asks us to let go of what is hindering us and trust the Spirit to bring about lasting change. Spend time in self-reflection. What is one habit, fear, or mindset that the Holy Spirit is urging you to release? Pray for the strength to let go and invite Him to shape you into Christ's likeness.

Prayer: Lord, I surrender my heart to You. Transform me through Your Spirit and help me to walk in a way that glorifies You. Teach me to reflect Your love, grace, and truth in all I do. Amen.

Overflowing with Hope
SUNDAY, 29 JUNE 2025

"But Those Who Hope in The Lord Will Renew Their Strength. They Will Soar on Wings Like Eagles; They Will Run and Not Grow Weary, They Will Walk and Not Be Faint." – Isaiah 40:31

"May The God of Hope Fill You with All Joy and Peace as You Trust in Him, So That You May Overflow with Hope by The Power of The Holy Spirit." – Romans 15:13

Biblical hope is a steady anchor, unshaken by the storms of life. It's not wishful thinking but confident assurance in the character and promises of God. This hope doesn't just sustain us; it overflows, touching the lives of those around us. C.S. Lewis described hope as a forward-looking virtue, pointing us toward the eternal reality of God's Kingdom. This perspective shifts our focus from the trials of today to the glory that awaits us. Through the Holy Spirit, this hope fuels joy and peace, no matter the circumstances. Identify one area where hopelessness has taken root in your life. Surrender it to God in prayer. Then, encourage someone else with a word of hope or a testimony of God's faithfulness. Let your hope inspire theirs.

Prayer: Father, thank You for being the God of hope. Fill my heart with joy and peace as I trust in You. Let my life overflow with hope, shining as a light in the lives of others. Amen.

Walking in Freedom
MONDAY, 30 JUNE 2025

"I Will Walk About in Freedom, For I Have Sought Out Your Precepts." – Psalm 119:45

"Now The Lord Is the Spirit, And Where the Spirit of The Lord Is, There Is Freedom." – 2 Corinthians 3:17

The freedom found in Christ is holistic. It is freedom from the chains of sin, freedom from the weight of shame and fear, and freedom to live boldly for His glory. This freedom isn't earned, it is a gift, secured by Christ and activated by the Spirit in our lives. Are there burdens you're carrying today? Anxiety, guilt, or the pressure to measure up? Release them to the Holy Spirit. Freedom in Christ means resting in His grace, knowing that His power is greater than any stronghold. Walk boldly, knowing that you are fully loved and fully free. Reflect on what may be holding you back be it fear, guilt, or comparison. Surrender it to the Holy Spirit, declaring freedom in Christ. Step into the day with confidence, knowing you are walking in His truth.

Prayer: Holy Spirit, thank You for the freedom You have given me. Help me to live daily in that freedom, unshackled by fear or shame, and empowered to fulfil Your purpose for my life. Amen.

JULY 2025

A Divine Promise
Tuesday,1 July 2025

"And I Will Ask the Father, And He Will Give You Another Helper, To Be with You Forever—Even the Spirit of Truth, Whom the World Cannot Receive, Because It Neither Sees Him nor Knows Him. You Know Him, For He Dwells with You and Will Be in You." – John 14:16-17

The Holy Spirit is not just a force or influence; He is a divine Person, and the Helper Jesus promised His followers. He is God's gift to every believer, guiding, comforting, and empowering us in our journey of faith. While the world may struggle to grasp His presence, we are invited to know Him personally and intimately. Take time today to acknowledge the Spirit as your constant companion. Let His presence remind you that you are never alone and that He is actively working in and through you. How aware are you of the Holy Spirit's presence in your daily life? Take a moment to thank Him for walking alongside you.

Prayer: Holy Spirit, thank You for dwelling within me. Help me to grow in awareness of Your presence and to lean on Your guidance each day. Amen.

A New Heart, A New Spirit
Wednesday, 2 July 2025

"I Will Give You a New Heart and Put a New Spirit in You; I Will Remove from You Your Heart of Stone and Give You a Heart of Flesh. And I Will Put My Spirit in You and Move You to Follow My Decrees and Be Careful to Keep My Laws." – Ezekiel 36:26-27

Through the Holy Spirit, God transforms us from within. He softens hardened hearts, renews our spirits, and empowers us to live in obedience to His will. This is not a change we accomplish by our own effort but one made possible through His Spirit dwelling in us. Today, reflect on areas where your heart may feel resistant or hardened. Invite the Spirit to renew and soften those areas, enabling you to walk in alignment with God's purpose. Are there parts of your heart or life where you've resisted change? Surrender them to God and allow the Spirit to work.

Prayer: Lord, give me a new heart and renew my spirit. Help me to walk faithfully in Your ways as You transform me from the inside out. Amen.

The Helper in Times of Need
Thursday, 3 July 2025

"But the Advocate, the Holy Spirit, whom the Father will send in my name, will teach you all things and will remind you of everything I have said to you. – John 14:26

Life often presents us with moments of uncertainty and confusion, but the Holy Spirit is our divine Helper and Advocate - the *Parakletos* in Greek, meaning 'Comforter.' He gently reminds us of God's truth and leads us forward with unwavering guidance. As our teacher, the Spirit illuminates Scripture, providing clarity and equipping us with wisdom to navigate life's challenges. Take time today to meditate on God's Word. Invite the Holy Spirit to reveal fresh insights, to deepen your understanding, and to guide your decisions. Trust in His perfect timing. He will provide exactly what you need, precisely when you need it. Are there areas in your life where you feel uncertain or lost? How can you welcome the Spirit into those situations? Place your trust in His teaching and guidance, knowing He will never fail you.

Prayer: Holy Spirit, thank You for being my Helper. Open my eyes to Your truth and teach me to trust Your guidance in every situation. Amen.

Developing a Relationship with the Spirit
Friday, 4 July 2025

"Do You Not Know That Your Bodies Are Temples of The Holy Spirit, Who Is in You, Whom You Have Received from God? You Are Not Your Own." – 1 Corinthians 6:19

The Holy Spirit dwells within us, making us living temples of God's presence. Developing a personal relationship with Him means acknowledging His indwelling presence and engaging with Him through prayer, worship, and obedience. He desires to be more than a distant force; He wants to walk closely with us every day. Consider ways to deepen your relationship with the Spirit today. Whether through prayer, quiet reflection, or worship, invite Him to fill every part of your life. How can you make space in your life to nurture a closer relationship with the Holy Spirit?

Prayer: Holy Spirit, I invite You to take up residence in my life. Help me to honour Your presence and to seek a deeper relationship with You each day. Amen.

The Spirit's Role in Our Growth
Saturday, 5 July 2025

"For God Has Not Given Us a Spirit of Fear, But of Power and Of Love and Of a Sound Mind." – 2 Timothy 1:7 NKJV

Fear can paralyse and prevent us from stepping into the abundant life God has prepared for us. During a time of severe persecution, Paul wrote these words to Timothy, reminding him that fear does not come from God. Timothy faced challenges within and beyond the church, yet Paul encouraged him to rely on the Spirit. Through the Holy Spirit, God equips us with *Power*, *Love*, and a *Sound Mind*. His power gives strength to endure and overcome challenges. His love drives out fear, replacing it with courage to serve others selflessly. His gift of a sound mind brings clarity, self-discipline, and calm amidst life's pressures. Today, reflect on areas where fear grips your heart. Invite the Spirit to fill you with courage, enabling you to move forward boldly in faith. Trust that God has already given you the tools to break free from fear and live confidently in Him.

Prayer: Lord, thank You for Your Spirit. Fill me with power, love, and a sound mind. Help me walk boldly in Your purpose. Amen.

Growing in Awareness of His Presence
SUNDAY, 6 JULY 2025

"The Spirit of God Has Made Me; The Breath of The Almighty Gives Me Life." – Job 33:4

The Holy Spirit is alive and active! He is not a distant force or a fleeting moment but a constant, empowering presence in your life. His breath fills your lungs; His power moves through you. Growing in awareness of His presence isn't just an abstract concept, it is stepping into the divine reality that the Spirit is with you, within you, and working through you every second of every day. Pause and sense Him now. Look for His fingerprints in the sunrise, hear His whispers in the stillness, and feel His touch through the peace that surpasses understanding. You are not alone - the Spirit of the Living God is at work in your ordinary moments, turning them into extraordinary opportunities to encounter Him. Cultivate a lifestyle of Holy Spirit awareness. Speak to Him, invite Him to lead, and expect Him to move mightily in every aspect of your life. This is the power of walking hand in hand with the Spirit.

Prayer: Holy Spirit, I thank You that You are always with me. Awaken my senses to Your presence. Lead me, guide me, and empower me to walk boldly in step with You. Come, Holy Spirit, come! Amen.

Empowered for Witnessing
MONDAY, 7 JULY 2025

"But You Will Receive Power When the Holy Spirit Comes on You; And You Will Be My Witnesses in Jerusalem, And in All Judea and Samaria, And to The Ends of The Earth." – Acts 1:8

The power of the Holy Spirit transforms ordinary lives into vessels of extraordinary impact. Jesus didn't promise earthly accolades or prestige He promised divine power to proclaim His message. This power isn't a result of mere attendance at church or participation in rituals; it flows from the Spirit's indwelling presence. I recall witnessing this truth during one of Rev. Reinhard Bonnke's gospel crusades in Nigeria. He likened the Spirit's work to transformation, saying, "Sitting in a garage doesn't make you a car." True transformation, and the boldness to witness, comes only through the Holy Spirit. This power is not confined to monumental events but is available every day through your words, actions, and the way you live. The Spirit enables you to reflect God's love, even when faced with opposition. Where can you bear witness today? Ask the Spirit to strengthen you with boldness, compassion, and faithfulness to fulfil your divine mission.

Prayer: Holy Spirit, thank You for Your power at work in me. Fill me with boldness to share Christ's love, and let my life testify to Your goodness. Amen.

God's Strength in Our Weakness
TUESDAY, 8 JULY 2025

"But He Said to Me, 'My Grace Is Sufficient for You, For My Power Is Made Perfect in Weakness.'" – 2 Corinthians 12:9

Your weaknesses are not obstacles to God's plans, they are opportunities for His power to shine. The Holy Spirit takes your vulnerabilities and transforms them into testimonies of His strength. In moments of inadequacy, lean fully on the Spirit and watch Him work through you in ways you never imagined. Embrace your weaknesses today, knowing that God's grace is more than enough. Trust that He is moulding you for His divine purposes, even through your struggles. His power will be perfected in you as you surrender and rely on Him completely.

Prayer: Lord, thank You for displaying Your strength through my weaknesses. Help me to rely on Your Spirit and trust in Your sufficient grace. Amen.

Not by Might, Nor by Power
WEDNESDAY, 9 JULY 2025

"'Not By Might nor By Power, But by My Spirit,' Says the Lord Almighty." – Zechariah 4:6

The challenges we face cannot be overcome by human strength alone, they require the Spirit's divine power. Zerubbabel faced an immense task, yet God reminded him that success would come not through his own abilities but through the Holy Spirit's empowerment. Reflect on an area of your life where you've relied on your own strength. Surrender it to God and invite the Spirit to take control. Trust Him to lead you and accomplish what you cannot do on your own. Let His power be your strength today.

Prayer: Holy Spirit, teach me to rely on Your strength. Help me to surrender my efforts and trust in Your power to accomplish what I cannot. Amen.

Boldness in Sharing the Gospel
Thursday, 10 July 2025

"Declare His Glory Among the Nations, His Marvellous Works Among All Peoples." – Psalm 96:3

The call to declare God's glory is not limited to distant lands, it begins in the ordinary rhythms of our lives. Every word, every act of kindness, and every testimony of God's goodness are opportunities to share His marvellous works with the world. The Holy Spirit empowers us to step out in boldness, turning fear into faith and hesitation into action. Consider the people in your life - your neighbours, colleagues, or friends - who may not yet know of God's love. Pray for opportunities to share His glory with them. Whether it's through speaking words of encouragement, reflecting His kindness, or simply living a life that testifies to His goodness, the Spirit will guide you. Let today be a day where His glory shines through you.

Prayer: Lord, give me the courage to declare Your glory in all I do. Holy Spirit, guide my words and actions so that others may see Your marvellous works through me. Amen.

Gifts for Service
FRIDAY, 11 JULY 2025

"Each Of You Should Use Whatever Gift You Have Received to Serve Others, As Faithful Stewards of God's Grace in Its Various Forms." – 1 Peter 4:10

The Holy Spirit has uniquely equipped you with gifts to serve others and glorify God. These gifts are not for personal recognition but to build His kingdom and reveal His love to the world. Take time today to reflect on the ways God has gifted you. How can you use these gifts to bless others in your home, church, or community? Trust the Spirit to guide and strengthen you as you step out in service.

Prayer: Holy Spirit, thank You for the gifts You've given me. Help me to use them faithfully to serve others and bring glory to Your name. Amen.

Guided by the Spirit
SATURDAY, 12 JULY 2025

"When The Spirit of Truth Comes, He Will Guide You into All the Truth." – John 16:13

The Holy Spirit is your divine navigator, cutting through the noise of life to bring clarity, wisdom, and peace. He doesn't leave you to wander aimlessly - He comes with truth, power, and purpose! Right now, the Spirit is present, ready to lead you in every decision and every step. Are you listening? Are you making room for Him to speak into your life? Pray, lean into His Word, and trust that He will reveal the path you need to take. When the Spirit speaks, mountains move, and doors open.

Prayer: Holy Spirit, thank You for guiding me into all truth. Sharpen my ears to hear Your voice and my heart to follow Your direction boldly. Amen.

Living for God's Glory
SUNDAY, 13 JULY 2025

"In The Same Way, Let Your Light Shine Before Others, That They May See Your Good Deeds and Glorify Your Father in Heaven." – Matthew 5:16

You were made to shine! The Holy Spirit has ignited a flame in you that reflects the glory of God to the world. Each act of kindness, word of encouragement, and moment of integrity is a beacon of hope that points to Jesus. The Spirit's power in you is unstoppable, lighting up even the darkest places. Today, ask the Holy Spirit to reveal how your life can proclaim God's goodness. Whether in your family, workplace, or community, walk boldly and let your light shine for His glory.

Prayer: Lord may my life blaze with Your glory. Holy Spirit, empower me to shine brightly, so others may encounter Your love and grace. Amen.

Equipped by the Spirit
MONDAY, 14 JULY 2025

"There Are Different Kinds of Gifts, But the Same Spirit Distributes Them." – 1 Corinthians 12:4

You are empowered by the Holy Spirit with divine gifts designed to impact the world and build God's kingdom. These aren't ordinary abilities they are supernatural tools to reveal His love, strengthen His Church, and demonstrate His power. Your unique gift is no accident; it's a part of God's extraordinary plan. Step out in faith today! Trust that the Spirit has equipped you for service, and He will multiply the impact of your gifts when you surrender them to His will.

Prayer: Holy Spirit, thank You for the gifts You have placed within me. Empower me to use them boldly, bringing glory to God and blessing those around me. Amen.

Unity in Diversity
TUESDAY, 15 JULY 2025

"How Good and Pleasant It Is When God's People Live Together in Unity!" – Psalm 133:1

The body of Christ is unstoppable when it moves in unity! The Holy Spirit knits together our unique gifts and callings, creating a powerful tapestry of grace. No gift is too small, and no person is overlooked - we are all vital in God's divine plan. Celebrate the diversity of God's people! Honour the gifts of those around you and seek ways to work together in harmony. When the Church operates as one, it becomes a blazing testimony to the world of God's love and glory.

Prayer: Lord, thank You for the beauty of unity in the body of Christ. Holy Spirit, teach me to value and support the gifts of others, so together we may reveal Your greatness. Amen.

Gifts for the Common Good
WEDNESDAY, 16 JULY 2025

"Now To Each One the Manifestation of The Spirit Is Given for The Common Good." – 1 Corinthians 12:7

The gifts of the Spirit are given to every believer, not for self-promotion, but for strengthening the body of Christ and revealing God's love to the world. Charles Spurgeon reminds us, *"You Are Not Your Own; You Are His. And The Gifts You Have Are Not Your Own; They Are His, Given to You to Glorify Him and Bless Others."* This truth calls us to humility, recognising that our gifts are tools to encourage, unify, and build others up. Today, ask the Spirit to show you how your gifts can bless someone else. Whether through a word of encouragement, an act of service, or even your silent prayers, your faithfulness can have an eternal impact.

Prayer: Holy Spirit, remind me that my gifts are for the common good. Teach me to serve others with humility and bring glory to Your name. Amen.

Discovering Your Spiritual Gifts
THURSDAY, 17 JULY 2025

"We Have Different Gifts, According to The Grace Given to Each of Us." – Romans 12:6

God has shaped each of us uniquely, equipping us with gifts that reflect His creative power and purpose. A.W. Tozer famously said, *"God Does Not Call the Qualified; He Qualifies the Called."* This means that discovering your gifts is not about striving, but about surrender and allowing the Spirit to reveal the unique ways you are meant to serve. Spend time today reflecting on what stirs your heart and energises your spirit. Often, it's in service and obedience that our gifts come to light. Pray for the Spirit to guide you as you step boldly into the purpose God has prepared for you.

Prayer: Lord, help me discover the gifts You've placed within me. Equip me to use them faithfully for Your glory and the benefit of others. Amen.

Serving with Love
FRIDAY, 18 JULY 2025

"If I Speak in The Tongues of Men or Of Angels, But Do Not Have Love, I Am Only a Resounding Gong or A Clanging Cymbal." – 1 Corinthians 13:1

Love is the lifeblood of spiritual gifts. Without it, even the most impressive abilities mean nothing. As David Livingstone once said, *"If A Commission by An Earthly King Is Considered an Honour, How Can a Commission by A Heavenly King Be Considered a Sacrifice?"* When we serve in the Spirit's love, our efforts become acts of worship, reflecting Christ's humility and compassion. Who can you bless today? Let love drive your service, allowing the Spirit to use you as a vessel of His grace and kindness. Even small actions, when fuelled by love, can have eternal impact.

Prayer: Lord, fill me with Your love as I serve. Holy Spirit, guide my words and actions to reflect Christ's heart in all I do. Amen.

Pursuing Unity
SATURDAY, 19 JULY 2025

"Make Every Effort to Keep the Unity of The Spirit Through the Bond of Peace." – Ephesians 4:3

Unity within the Church is a testimony of God's grace, but maintaining it takes intentionality and surrender to the Spirit. John Stott observed, *"Unity Without the Spirit Is Impossible; Unity Through the Spirit Is Unstoppable."* It is only by the Spirit's power that we can reconcile, forgive, and work together as one body. Are there broken relationships in your life? Pray for the Spirit to guide you in humility and courage. Take a step toward reconciliation today, trusting that God will bring peace and healing. Unity honours Christ and demonstrates His love to the world.

Prayer: Holy Spirit, help me to pursue unity in my relationships. Teach me to prioritise peace, forgiveness, and love, even when it's difficult. Amen.

Celebrating Unity in Diversity
SUNDAY, 20 JULY 2025

"Now You Are the Body of Christ, And Each One of You Is a Part of It." – 1 Corinthians 12:27

The Church is a vibrant tapestry, woven together by the Holy Spirit. Each thread, representing our unique gifts and callings, plays an essential role in reflecting God's glory to the world. In His infinite wisdom, God designed us to complement one another, strengthening His body through unity in diversity. Pause today to thank God for the way He has uniquely crafted you and those around you. Acknowledge and celebrate the contributions of others in your church or community, remembering that together, we are the hands and feet of Christ.

Prayer: Lord, thank You for making us one body. Help me honour the gifts of others and serve joyfully in my place within Your perfect design. Amen.

Rooted in His Life-Giving Spirit
MONDAY, 21 JULY 2025

"The Fruit of The Righteous Is a Tree of Life, And the One Who Is Wise Saves Lives." – Proverbs 11:30

The Holy Spirit transforms our lives into sources of life and hope for others. Like a tree deeply rooted in fertile soil, a Spirit-filled life bears fruit that nourishes and inspires everyone it touches. Through our actions, words, and example, we become living testimonies of God's grace and goodness. Consider how your life can bring encouragement and wisdom to others today. Look for opportunities to reflect Christ's love in even the smallest interactions, allowing His Spirit to work through you.

Prayer: Holy Spirit, make my life a tree of life that blesses others. Help me to stay rooted in You, bearing fruit that glorifies Your name. Amen.

Living Love Out Loud
TUESDAY, 22 JULY 2025

"But The Fruit of The Spirit Is Love, Joy, Peace, Forbearance, Kindness, Goodness, Faithfulness." – Galatians 5:22

Love is not passive; it is active, visible, and transformative. The Holy Spirit fills us with the kind of love that moves beyond words, touching lives and breaking down barriers. This love mirrors Christ's sacrifice and compels us to serve those in need, even when it's uncomfortable or inconvenient. Today, let your actions proclaim the love of Christ. Whether it's through a small gesture of kindness or a deliberate act of service, ask the Spirit to use you as a vessel of His perfect love.

Prayer: Lord, fill my heart with Your love and teach me to live it out boldly. May my life be a reflection of Your heart for the world. Amen.

Joy in His Presence
WEDNESDAY, 23 JULY 2025

"You Make Known to Me the Path of Life; You Will Fill Me with Joy in Your Presence, With Eternal Pleasures at Your Right Hand." – Psalm 16:11

Joy is not dependent on circumstances; it is rooted in the unchanging presence of God. The Holy Spirit fills us with a deep, abiding joy that sustains us through life's highs and lows. This verse, brimming with promise, was a favourite of Kathryn Kuhlman, the renowned evangelist whose ministry was defined by her intimacy with the Spirit. I vividly remember encountering her story and teachings for the first time as a new believer. Reading about her life and hearing her words felt like stepping into a realm of faith and wonder I had never experienced before. Her 1969 book, *God Can Do It Again*, mesmerised me with its incredible accounts of God's power. Honestly, I don't think I've ever fully recovered from the impact. Her life was a testimony of the joy and transformation that flows from living completely surrendered to the Spirit's presence. Take a moment today to reflect on God's goodness. Let the Spirit renew your heart with joy as you remember His blessings and faithfulness. May we always stand in awe of the joy found in His presence.

Prayer: Holy Spirit, thank You for filling me with joy that cannot be shaken. Help me to live in Your presence and reflect that joy to others. Amen.

Carried by His Peace
THURSDAY, 24 JULY 2025

"Peace I Leave With You; My Peace I Give You. I Do Not Give to You as The World Gives. Do Not Let Your Hearts Be Troubled and Do Not Be Afraid." – John 14:27

True peace cannot be found in circumstances, it is a gift of the Spirit that calms our hearts even in life's storms. This peace anchors us in the knowledge that God is in control, enabling us to face challenges with faith and confidence. If you feel overwhelmed or anxious today, take a deep breath and lay your burdens at God's feet. Invite the Spirit to fill your heart with His peace, and let His presence remind you that you are held by the Almighty.

Prayer: Lord, thank You for Your peace that surpasses all understanding. Help me to trust You fully and to reflect Your peace to those around me. Amen.

Persevering with Patience
FRIDAY, 25 JULY 2025

"But If We Hope for What We Do Not Yet Have, We Wait for It Patiently." – Romans 8:25

Patience is not passive resignation; it is a Spirit-enabled endurance that trusts God's timing in all things. It's the kind of patience that transforms waiting into worship, knowing that God is always at work for our good. Today, choose to rest in His promises. Whether you are waiting for an answer, a breakthrough, or a change, trust that His plans are worth the wait. The Spirit will strengthen you to endure with grace and hope.

Prayer: Holy Spirit, help me to wait on You with a heart full of trust. Teach me to see the beauty in Your timing and to reflect Your peace in every season. Amen.

Radiating Kindness and Goodness
SATURDAY, 26 JULY 2025

"Be Kind and Compassionate To One Another, Forgiving Each Other, Just as In Christ God Forgave You." – Ephesians 4:32

Kindness flows naturally from a heart filled with the Spirit. It is a reflection of God's character, bringing light to even the darkest situations. When we show kindness and goodness to others, we reflect the love that Christ has lavished on us. Look for opportunities today to extend kindness whether it's through a word of encouragement, an act of generosity, or a moment of forgiveness. Trust that even small acts can make a big difference in someone's life.

Prayer: Lord, let Your kindness overflow through me today. Help me to see others through Your eyes and respond with compassion and grace. Amen.

A Life of Faithfulness
SUNDAY, 27 JULY 2025

"Let Love and Faithfulness Never Leave You; Bind Them Around Your Neck, Write Them on The Tablet of Your Heart." – Proverbs 3:3

Faithfulness is a quiet strength that anchors us in God's promises, enabling us to remain steadfast even when the road is long. It is the Spirit's work in us, cultivating a heart that honours commitments and reflects God's unwavering love. Today, ask the Spirit to deepen your faithfulness whether in your relationships, responsibilities, or walk with Him. Through His power, you can reflect the constancy of God's love to those around you.

Prayer: Holy Spirit, make me faithful in all that I do. Help me to honour You through my words and actions, and to reflect Your character in every season. Amen.

Led by the Spirit
Monday, 28 July 2025

"For Those Who Are Led by The Spirit of God Are the Children of God." – Romans 8:14

The Holy Spirit leads us as children of God, guiding us in decisions, relationships, and our walk with Christ. His guidance is not forced but gentle, inviting us to follow Him in faith. By trusting the Spirit, we grow deeper in our identity as God's children and align our lives with His will. Take time today to ask the Spirit to lead you. Whether in small decisions or major life choices, trust that He will show you the way.

Prayer: Holy Spirit, thank You for leading me as a child of God. Teach me to trust Your guidance and to follow where You lead. Amen.

Hearing His Voice
TUESDAY, 29 JULY 2025

"Whether You Turn to The Right or To the Left, Your Ears Will Hear a Voice Behind You, Saying, 'This Is the Way; Walk in It.'" – Isaiah 30:21

The Holy Spirit constantly speaks to us, guiding, encouraging, and directing our steps. In the midst of life's busyness and noise, His still, small voice calls us to pause and listen. As Smith Wigglesworth wisely put it, *"God Does Not Speak to Those Who Are in A Hurry. Stop, Wait, And Listen."* Take time today to quiet your surroundings and seek His voice. Through prayer and reflection, invite the Spirit to speak into your heart, and trust that He will show you the way to walk. His guidance is ever present and unfailing.

Prayer: Lord, quiet the noise in my life so I can hear Your voice. Teach me to listen carefully and follow the path You have lovingly set before me. Amen.

The Spirit of Truth
WEDNESDAY, 30 JULY 2025

"But When He, The Spirit of Truth, Comes, He Will Guide You into All the Truth." – John 16:13

The Holy Spirit, the Spirit of Truth, is our faithful guide through life's uncertainties. He doesn't merely reveal facts but leads us into the eternal truth of God's Word. Charles Spurgeon observed, *"Discernment Is Not Knowing the Difference Between Right and Wrong. It Is Knowing the Difference Between Right and Almost Right."* In a world clouded by confusion and competing voices, the Spirit brings clarity, illuminating the way forward. Today, ask Him to help you discern truth and align your heart with God's perfect will.

Prayer: Holy Spirit, thank You for being my guide into all truth. Open my eyes to see with clarity and grant me wisdom to walk in Your ways. Amen.

Walking in Step with the Spirit
THURSDAY, 31 JULY 2025

"Since We Live by The Spirit, Let Us Keep in Step with The Spirit." – Galatians 5:25

Walking in step with the Spirit means aligning your life with His will and responding to His promptings. This intentional journey requires daily surrender. As Catherine Booth once said, *"If We Are to Better the Future, We Must Disturb the Present."* Keeping in step with the Spirit often calls us to move beyond our comfort zones and embrace God's higher purposes. Pause throughout your day to reconnect with the Spirit. Pray for His guidance and be ready to respond to His leading. His way is always right, and His timing is always perfect.

Prayer: Lord, guide me to walk in step with Your Spirit today. Help my actions, thoughts, and decisions to reflect Your will and bring glory to Your name. Amen.

AUGUST 2025

Trusting God Through the Spirit
FRIDAY, 1 AUGUST 2025

"Trust In the Lord with All Your Heart and Lean Not on Your Own Understanding; In All Your Ways Submit to Him, And He Will Make Your Paths Straight." – Proverbs 3:5-6

Surrender is the ultimate act of faith. To trust the Holy Spirit's guidance is to release our grip on control, allowing God to take the lead. The Spirit often speaks into the spaces where our plans falter, gently reminding us that His ways are far higher than ours. God doesn't ask us to understand everything - He asks us to trust Him completely. He takes our willingness to submit, shaping it into a life guided by His perfect will. Today, bring the areas of uncertainty in your life before Him. Allow the Spirit to reframe your perspective and walk forward with confidence, knowing that He directs every step.

Prayer: Holy Spirit, I submit my plans and desires to You. Lead me with Your wisdom and teach me to trust You with all my heart, even in uncertainty. Amen.

Responding to His Call
SATURDAY, 2 AUGUST 2025

"Do Not Quench the Spirit." – 1 Thessalonians 5:19

The Spirit's voice often comes as a whisper, stirring us to action or drawing our attention to areas that need change. Ignoring His leading diminishes our sensitivity to His work in our lives. Have you felt Him nudge your heart recently? Perhaps He's calling you to reach out, to change course, or to step out in faith. Delayed obedience is still disobedience, but bold responsiveness leads to joy and purpose. The Spirit longs to work in and through you today. Will you answer His call?

Prayer: Lord, help me to respond without hesitation to the voice of Your Spirit. Keep my heart open and eager to obey, no matter the cost. Amen.

Living in the Light of His Word
SUNDAY, 3 AUGUST 2025

"Your Word Is a Lamp to My Feet and A Light for My Path." – Psalm 119:105

To live a Spirit-led life is to walk in the light of God's Word. The Spirit takes Scripture, applying it uniquely to the situations we face, offering wisdom, encouragement, and direction. Without His guidance, our steps can falter, but with Him, each step is grounded in truth and grace. Dedicate time today to read Scripture intentionally. Don't just read the words but invite the Spirit to speak through them. His presence transforms every page, turning it into a living guide for your journey.

Prayer: Holy Spirit, illuminate my path through the truth of Your Word. Speak into my heart and guide me to live in alignment with Your perfect will. Amen.

The Promise of the Comforter
MONDAY, 4 AUGUST 2025

"But The Comforter, Which Is the Holy Ghost, Whom the Father Will Send in My Name, He Shall Teach You All Things, And Bring All Things to Your Remembrance, Whatsoever I Have Said unto You." – John 14:26 (KJV)

Imagine this: Jesus, knowing His time on earth was drawing to an end, promised His disciples the Holy Spirit. He promised not just an abstract force but a living, active presence - the Comforter. This wasn't a mere consolation prize. It was the power and presence of God given to dwell within us, teaching, reminding, and strengthening us every step of the way. Have you embraced the fullness of this promise? Too often, we try to navigate life with human wisdom while neglecting the Spirit's counsel. Today, pause and invite the Comforter to guide you. What challenges or decisions do you face that require divine wisdom? Trust His leading. He never fails.

Prayer: Holy Spirit, thank You for being my Comforter and teacher. Open my heart to Your guidance and help me to walk in step with You today. Amen.

Unshakable Peace
TUESDAY, 5 AUGUST 2025

"And The Peace of God, Which Transcends All Understanding, Will Guard Your Hearts and Your Minds in Christ Jesus." – Philippians 4:7

There's a kind of peace that defies explanation. It's not the absence of trouble but a supernatural stillness that anchors us amidst the chaos. This is the peace the Holy Spirit offers not as the world gives, fleeting and circumstantial, but eternal and steadfast. Think of the storms you've faced recently. Did fear or frustration dominate, or did you allow the Spirit to guard your heart with His peace? Today, let go of every anxious thought. Lay your cares at Jesus' feet and ask the Holy Spirit to fill you with that unshakable peace.

Prayer: Lord, I surrender my worries to You. Holy Spirit, flood my heart and mind with Your peace and teach me to trust You completely. Amen.

A Healing Presence
WEDNESDAY, 6 AUGUST 2025

"The Lord Is Close to The Broken-hearted and Saves Those Who Are Crushed in Spirit." – Psalm 34:18

When grief and pain threaten to overwhelm, the Holy Spirit draws near with healing in His wings. He doesn't minimise your pain, He meets you in it, bringing the comfort that only God can give. The Spirit not only binds up broken hearts but uses our brokenness as a testimony of His restoring power. Is there a wound you've tried to hide from Him? Don't hold back. Lay it bare before the Spirit today and trust Him to bring healing in His perfect time and way.

Prayer: Holy Spirit, thank You for being close when my heart feels shattered. Help me to trust You with my pain and receive the healing only You can bring. Amen.

Empowered in Weakness
THURSDAY, 7 AUGUST 2025

"In The Same Way, The Spirit Helps Us in Our Weakness. We Do Not Know What We Ought to Pray For, But the Spirit Himself Intercedes for Us Through Wordless Groans." – Romans 8:26

How often do we strive to handle life's burdens in our own strength, only to find ourselves weary and discouraged? Yet, in our weakness, the Holy Spirit steps in not as a silent observer but as our active intercessor. He prays on our behalf, carrying our groans to the Father and strengthening us from within. Today, acknowledge your limitations and lean into His power. Even when words fail, trust that the Spirit knows your heart and is already working for your good.

Prayer: Lord, I am so grateful that Your Spirit intercedes for me. In my weakness, remind me that Your strength is more than enough. Amen.

Safe in His Arms
FRIDAY, 8 AUGUST 2025

"The Eternal God Is Your Refuge, And Underneath Are the Everlasting Arms." – Deuteronomy 33:27

There is no safer place than in the arms of God. The Holy Spirit cradles us when life feels unbearable, reminding us of the unfailing love of the Father. His everlasting arms are strong enough to carry us and gentle enough to heal us. What burdens are you carrying today? Let go of the need to control and allow the Spirit to lift you. Rest in the knowledge that God's arms are always open, ready to embrace and sustain you.

Prayer: Holy Spirit, thank You for carrying me when I'm too weary to walk. Help me to rest in Your strength and trust in Your unfailing care. Amen.

Agents of Comfort
SATURDAY, 9 AUGUST 2025

"Praise Be to The God and Father of Our Lord Jesus Christ, The Father of Compassion and The God of All Comfort, Who Comforts Us in All Our Troubles, So That We Can Comfort Those in Any Trouble with The Comfort We Ourselves Receive from God." – 2 Corinthians 1:3-4

The Spirit's work in our lives is not just for us; it's meant to overflow to others. As we experience His comfort, we are called to become agents of that same compassion, showing others the love and care we've received. Who in your life needs a touch of God's comfort today? Let the Holy Spirit guide you to be His hands and feet, bringing encouragement to those who are hurting.

Prayer: Lord, thank You for the comfort You've given me. Help me to share that comfort with others and be a vessel of Your love. Amen.

Soul Rest
SUNDAY, 10 AUGUST 2025

"Come To Me, All You Who Are Weary and Burdened, And I Will Give You Rest." – Matthew 11:28

The invitation to rest in Jesus is one of the most beautiful gifts we have. Through the Holy Spirit, we are drawn to the place of rest not a temporary escape, but a deep refreshment for our souls. It's here that we lay down every burden, every worry, and every fear, and find peace in His presence. Are you carrying something today that feels too heavy? Jesus is waiting. Come to Him with open hands and a surrendered heart, and let the Spirit fill you with His renewal.

Prayer: Lord, I bring my burdens to You. Thank You for the rest and peace You offer through Your Spirit. Renew my strength and refresh my soul today. Amen.

Filled with the Spirit
Monday, 11 August 2025

"Do Not Get Drunk on Wine, Which Leads to Debauchery. Instead, Be Filled with The Spirit, Speaking To One Another With Psalms, Hymns, And Songs from The Spirit. Sing And Make Music from Your Heart to The Lord." – Ephesians 5:18-19

The Holy Spirit transforms our worship, filling our hearts with joy and gratitude as we praise God. When we worship in the Spirit, it becomes more than just a ritual it becomes an encounter with God's presence. Singing and making music from the heart invite the Spirit to move powerfully in and through us. Today, let your worship overflow from a heart that is filled with the Spirit. Whether through singing, praying, or serving, invite the Holy Spirit to make your worship an offering to God.

Prayer: Holy Spirit, fill my heart with joy as I worship You. Let my praise come from a place of love and gratitude, and may it glorify Your name. Amen.

A Life of Worship
Tuesday, 12 August 2025

"Let Everything That Has Breathe Praise the Lord. Praise The Lord." – Psalm 150:6

Worship is not limited to singing in church it is a way of life. Every breath we take is an opportunity to praise God for His goodness and grace. The Holy Spirit enables us to live in constant worship, honouring God through our words, actions, and choices. Take time today to offer praise to God, not only in your words but also in how you live. Let each moment, big or small, reflect gratitude to Him.

Prayer: Lord, I want my life to be an act of worship to You. Teach me to praise You in all I do, and let the Spirit lead me in worship every day. Amen.

Worship in Spirit and Power
WEDNESDAY, 13 AUGUST 2025

"But The Hour Is Coming, And Is Now Here, When the True Worshippers Will Worship the Father in Spirit and Truth, For the Father Is Seeking Such People to Worship Him." – John 4:23

True worship isn't confined to a church building or a certain style of music. It springs from hearts surrendered to God, filled with the Holy Spirit, and anchored in His truth. When we worship in Spirit and power, something extraordinary happens, our hearts align with heaven, and the presence of God transforms us. Do you worship God out of routine or out of a deep connection with Him? Reflect on what authentic worship means in your life. The Spirit desires to guide you into worship that honours God and fuels your faith. Set aside a dedicated moment today to worship God wholeheartedly. Let the Holy Spirit guide your prayers, praise, or quiet meditation.

Prayer: Holy Spirit, empower me to worship God with all my heart. Let my worship be pleasing to You and transform me to reflect Your glory. Amen.

The Spirit of Renewal
THURSDAY, 14 AUGUST 2025

"He Saved Us Through the Washing of Rebirth and Renewal by The Holy Spirit." – Titus 3:5

The Holy Spirit renews us not just once, but daily. He breathes new life into weary souls, clears away doubt, and refreshes us with His peace and power. Renewal means being shaped into Christ's likeness, restored to walk boldly in His purposes. Are there areas in your life that feel stagnant or drained? Invite the Holy Spirit to renew your strength, your joy, and your passion for God's calling. Allow Him to transform your outlook as you surrender to His work in you. Take five minutes to be still in God's presence. Invite the Spirit to renew your heart and renew areas in which you've felt tired or distant from Him.

Prayer: Lord, pour out Your Spirit of renewal in my life. Refresh my heart, restore my strength, and ignite my passion for You. Amen.

The Spirit Who Gives Wisdom
FRIDAY, 15 AUGUST 2025

"The Spirit of The Lord Will Rest on Him - The Spirit of Wisdom and Understanding, The Spirit of Counsel and Might, The Spirit of The Knowledge and Fear of The Lord." – Isaiah 11:2

Wisdom is not merely knowledge or intellect; it is the ability to discern and act according to God's will. The Holy Spirit is the source of divine wisdom, guiding us in decisions big and small. He helps us navigate life with clarity and grace, bringing understanding to situations that confuse the world. Do you have a decision or challenge that requires God's wisdom? Ask the Spirit for guidance and trust that He will direct your steps. Bring a specific area of decision-making or confusion to the Holy Spirit in prayer. Write down any Scriptures or impressions He places on your heart.

Prayer: Holy Spirit, fill me with Your wisdom and understanding. Help me to see clearly and choose rightly in alignment with Your will. Amen.

The Spirit's Peace
SATURDAY, 16 AUGUST 2025

"And The Peace of God, Which Transcends All Understanding, Will Guard Your Hearts and Your Minds in Christ Jesus." – Philippians 4:7

The Holy Spirit brings us into a peace that surpasses all comprehension. It's a divine calm that steadies us, even when life feels uncertain or chaotic. This peace is not the absence of trouble but the assurance of God's presence in every situation. Today, ask the Spirit to fill your heart with this peace. Let it guard you against worry and fear and remind you that God's hand is over your life. Take a moment to sit quietly in prayer. As you breathe deeply, surrender every worry to the Spirit and invite His peace to fill your heart and mind.

Prayer: Holy Spirit, fill me with Your peace that surpasses understanding. Guard my heart from fear and remind me that You are my refuge in every season. Amen.

The Spirit Who Leads
SUNDAY, 17 AUGUST 2025

"For Those Who Are Led by The Spirit of God Are the Children of God." – Romans 8:14

Life is full of choices and paths, but the Spirit promises to guide us according to God's perfect will. His leadership isn't forceful, but it is gentle, rooted in love and truth. The more we surrender to the Joly Spirit's leading, the more we step into the fullness of our identity as God's children. Are you relying on your own understanding, or are you allowing the Spirit to lead you? Trust Him today to take you where you need to be, even if it feels unexpected or unfamiliar. Choose a specific decision or area in your life and intentionally ask the Spirit for His guidance. Write down how you sense Him directing you.

Prayer: Holy Spirit, lead me today in every decision and step. Help me trust Your guidance as a child of God, knowing You have my best in mind. Amen.

The Spirit of Transformation
MONDAY, 18 AUGUST 2025

"And We All, Who with Unveiled Faces Contemplate the Lord's Glory, Are Being Transformed into His Image with Ever-Increasing Glory, Which Comes from The Lord, Who Is the Spirit." – 2 Corinthians 3:18

Transformation is at the very heart of the Holy Spirit's work in our lives. He moulds us, shaping our character, attitudes, and desires to align more closely with Christ. This isn't a one-time event but an ongoing journey of surrender, as the Spirit works to reflect the glory of God through us. Where is the Spirit inviting you to grow or change today? Trust His gentle hand to lead you into greater freedom and Christlikeness. Reflect on an area in your life where you sense God is calling you to grow. Ask the Holy Spirit to guide you in letting go of old habits and embracing His transformative power.

Prayer: Holy Spirit, I surrender to Your transforming work in my life. Shape me into the likeness of Christ and let Your glory shine through me in all that I do. Amen.

Renewed Strength for the Weary
Tuesday, 19 August 2025

"He Gives Strength to The Weary and Increases the Power of The Weak. Even Youths Grow Tired and Weary, And Young Men Stumble and Fall; But Those Who Hope in The Lord Will Renew Their Strength. They Will Soar on Wings Like Eagles; They Will Run and Not Grow Weary, They Will Walk and Not Be Faint."
— Isaiah 40:29-31

When life feels overwhelming, the Holy Spirit offers strength and renewal. He meets us in our weariness and lifts us, giving us the energy and endurance to keep going. This strength doesn't come from our own effort but from placing our hope and trust in God. If you feel tired today, take a moment to rest in God's presence. Allow the Spirit to refresh and renew your heart.

Prayer: Lord, I am weary and need Your strength. Holy Spirit, renew my energy and help me to trust in Your sustaining power. Amen.

God's Power in Our Weakness
Wednesday, 20 August 2025

"But He Said to Me, 'My Grace Is Sufficient for You, For My Power Is Made Perfect in Weakness.' Therefore I Will Boast All The More Gladly About My Weaknesses, So That Christ's Power May Rest On Me." – 2 Corinthians 12:9

Our weaknesses are not a barrier to God's work—they are opportunities for His power to shine. The Holy Spirit uses our moments of struggle to reveal His grace and strength. When we rely on Him instead of our own abilities, His power becomes evident in our lives. Surrender your weaknesses to the Spirit today and trust Him to work through them for God's glory.

Prayer: Holy Spirit, thank You for being strong in my weakness. Help me to lean on Your grace and to trust in Your power when I feel inadequate. Amen.

Empowered by the Spirit's Hope
THURSDAY, 21 AUGUST 2025

"May The God of Hope Fill You with All Joy and Peace as You Trust in Him, So That You May Overflow with Hope by The Power of The Holy Spirit." – Romans 15:13

True hope isn't wishful thinking it is a steadfast anchor for our souls, rooted in the character and promises of God. The Holy Spirit doesn't just inspire hope; He sustains it, filling us with supernatural joy and peace that empower us to persevere. In a world often clouded by despair, this Spirit-empowered hope overflows, spilling into the lives of others. What part of your life feels devoid of hope? The Holy Spirit is ready to fill even the empty corners with His life-giving power. Trust in Him and allow His hope to rise within you. Identify an area of your life where you feel hope is lacking. Ask the Spirit to ignite fresh hope and reach out to encourage someone who may be struggling as well.

Prayer: Holy Spirit, fill me with hope that overflows. Help me to trust in God's promises and to be a beacon of encouragement for others. Amen.

Living in Spirit-Filled Grace
FRIDAY, 22 AUGUST 2025

"But You Are Not Controlled by The Sinful Nature. You Are Controlled by The Spirit If You Have the Spirit of God Living in You." – Romans 8:9

Grace doesn't just save us; it empowers us to live victoriously. The Holy Spirit gives us the strength to overcome sin and walk in freedom, reflecting the beauty of God's character. Grace is the Spirit's gift, enabling us to choose righteousness not through our own effort, but through His indwelling power. Are there areas where you feel powerless to change? Invite the Spirit to take control. His grace is sufficient to break chains and lead you into a life that glorifies God. Reflect on one area in which you're struggling to walk in God's way. Surrender it to the Spirit and choose one step of faith to walk in His freedom today.

Prayer: Holy Spirit, thank You for empowering me to live by grace. Take control of my life and help me to reflect Christ in all I do. Amen.

Finding Rest in the Spirit
SATURDAY, 23 AUGUST 2025

"Come To Me, All You Who Are Weary and Burdened, And I Will Give You Rest." – Matthew 11:28

We live in a restless world, constantly striving and rarely still. Yet the Holy Spirit invites us to find rest not just physical, but spiritual rest that refreshes our souls and renews our strength. He draws us into the presence of Jesus, where striving ceases and grace flows freely. Are you carrying burdens you were never meant to bear? Lay them at the feet of Christ and let the Holy Spirit minister to your heart with His peace and renewal. Carve out 10 minutes today to sit in silence with God. Bring your burdens before Him and ask the Spirit to help you release them into His care.

Prayer: Holy Spirit, lead me into the rest that only Jesus provides. Help me to surrender my striving and receive Your peace. Amen.

Renewed by the Spirit's Strength
SUNDAY, 24 AUGUST 2025

"Therefore We Do Not Lose Heart. Though Outwardly We Are Wasting Away, Yet Inwardly We Are Being Renewed Day by Day." – 2 Corinthians 4:16

The Spirit's work of renewal is a daily gift. He strengthens us when we are weak, refreshes us when we feel drained, and realigns us with God's promises when life becomes overwhelming. This renewal is not a one-time event but an ongoing process as we journey with Him. Have you been feeling weary? Trust the Spirit to renew you not through outward circumstances but by transforming you from the inside out. Begin your day with a prayer of surrender, asking the Holy Spirit to refresh your heart and strengthen your spirit for the challenges ahead.

Prayer: Holy Spirit, renew my heart and mind today. Fill me with Your strength and help me to walk in Your joy and peace. Amen.

Walking Freely by the Spirit
MONDAY, 25 AUGUST 2025

"I Will Walk About in Freedom, For I Have Sought Out Your Precepts." – Psalm 119:45

Freedom in the Spirit is not just deliverance from sin, it is the empowerment to live a life that honours God. The Holy Spirit frees us from the weight of guilt, fear, and shame, enabling us to walk confidently in God's love and truth. Is there an area of your life where you feel bound? Lay it before the Spirit and trust Him to lead you into the freedom that comes from walking in God's Word. Reflect on one area of your life where you feel constrained, whether by fear, guilt, or insecurity. Pray over it and declare the Spirit's freedom.

Prayer: Holy Spirit, thank You for the freedom found in Your truth. Help me to walk confidently and boldly as I follow Your guidance. Amen.

Breaking Chains with the Spirit
TUESDAY, 26 AUGUST 2025

"Now The Lord Is the Spirit, And Where the Spirit of The Lord Is, There Is Freedom." – 2 Corinthians 3:17

The presence of the Holy Spirit brings liberation and freedom from the chains of sin, fear, and lies that seek to hold us captive. His truth breaks every stronghold, and His power empowers us to live as beloved children of God. What is holding you back from experiencing true freedom? Ask the Spirit to reveal and break any chains and declare His victory over your life. Journal about an area where you long to experience freedom. Pray over it, asking the Holy Spirit to break through and bring healing and deliverance.

Prayer: Holy Spirit, thank You for breaking every chain. Help me to walk boldly in the freedom You provide and to live as a reflection of Your power. Amen.

The Spirit's Breath of Life
WEDNESDAY, 27 AUGUST 2025

"I Will Put My Spirit in You and You Will Live." – Ezekiel 37:14

The Holy Spirit breathes life into what feels dry and lifeless. Just as God revived the dry bones in Ezekiel's vision, the Holy Spirit can bring renewal to your heart, dreams, or circumstances. His power transforms what seems hopeless into a testimony of His glory. What feels stagnant or lifeless in your life? Invite the Spirit to breathe His life into it, trusting that His power is more than enough to bring restoration and renewal. Meditate on Ezekiel 37. Ask the Holy Spirit to identify an area in your life where He desires to breathe new life and pray over it boldly.

Prayer: Holy Spirit, breathe Your life into me. Renew my heart, restore my hope, and bring transformation to the areas that feel lifeless. Amen.

Liberation from Shame
Friday, 29 August 2025

"Therefore, There Is Now No Condemnation for Those Who Are in Christ Jesus." – Romans 8:1

A few years ago, during a series of sermons on the Holy Spirit - I believe it was during the COVID period - I shared this thought: *"The Holy Spirit Frees Us from The Power of Sin, But Jesus Frees Us from The Guilt of Sin."* It is through the Spirit that we are liberated from the weight of shame and guilt. Jesus' sacrifice has wiped the slate clean, and the Spirit continually reminds us of our identity as forgiven and cherished children of God. This gift of freedom enables us to move forward without being shackled by the mistakes of the past. Today, I encourage you to release any shame or guilt that you may still be carrying. Allow the Holy Spirit to affirm your forgiveness in Christ and walk boldly in the truth of His grace.

Prayer: Holy Spirit, thank You for setting me free from condemnation. Help me to live in the truth of who I am in Christ and leave shame behind. May my life reflect the freedom I have in You. Amen.

Transformed by His Presence
Saturday, 30 August 2025

"And We All, Who with Unveiled Faces Contemplate the Lord's Glory, Are Being Transformed into His Image with Ever-Increasing Glory, Which Comes from The Lord, Who Is the Spirit." – 2 Corinthians 3:18

The Holy Spirit works continuously to transform us into Christ's image. This transformation is not instant but a journey of surrender, growth, and renewal. As we fix our eyes on God's glory, the Spirit shapes us to reflect His love, grace, and truth. Reflect today on how the Spirit is transforming your character. Embrace this ongoing process and trust that He is shaping you for His glory.

Prayer: Holy Spirit, thank You for transforming me day by day. Help me to surrender to Your work in my life and to reflect Christ in all I do. Amen.

Freedom to Hope
Sunday, 31 August 2025

"You Will Know the Truth, And the Truth Will Set You Free." – John 8:32

The truth of God's Word, revealed by the Spirit, sets us free to live with hope and purpose. The Spirit's guidance liberates us from lies, fear, and doubt, anchoring us instead in the truth of God's promises. This freedom fills us with courage to face the future with confidence in His plans. Take a moment to reflect on how the Spirit's truth has set you free. Celebrate His work in your life and encourage others by sharing your story of hope and transformation.

Prayer: Lord, thank You for setting me free through Your truth. Holy Spirit, help me to walk boldly in this freedom and to share the hope I've found with others. Amen.

FINAL REFLECTIONS

Thank you for joining us on this journey through Deeply Rooted, crafted to nurture your faith and draw you closer to God. It is my hope that these pages have enriched your spiritual walk, unveiling the depth of His promises, wisdom, and unending love.

Each reflection has been thoughtfully prepared to guide you in prayer, meditation, and engagement with Scripture, offering strength and encouragement for your daily life. My prayer is that you remain firmly rooted in Christ, growing in faith, gratitude, and joy. As you continue to explore God's Word, may His love sustain and nourish your soul.

Whether you are embarking on your journey of faith or seeking to deepen your relationship with God, I trust this devotional has inspired and uplifted you. May it remain a source of encouragement, equipping you to live boldly in His truth and grace.

If you would like to receive future editions of Deeply Rooted, please fill out the form below and share your details with us. *We value your privacy and are committed to safeguarding your personal information. In compliance with GDPR regulations, your data will only be used for sharing devotional materials and updates. It will never be shared with third parties without your explicit consent.*

It is a blessing to support you on your spiritual journey and to grow together in faith.

In grace and gratitude,

Henry

Mailing List Sign-Up Form

Name: _____

Email Address: _____

Phone Number (Optional):_____

Mailing Address (Optional):_____

Preferred Format: (Check one)

- [ ] Email

- [ ] Printed Copy

- [ ] Both

Comments or Special Requests:

_____
_____
_____
_____

Please send the information by email to:
henryohakah@icloud.com

Or by post to:
**Mountsorrel Baptist Church
Leicester Road, Mountsorrel
Loughborough
LE12 7AJ**

ABOUT THE AUTHOR

Henry C. Ohakah brings a unique combination of experience and spiritual insight to his ministry. With a background in accounting and finance, Henry responded to God's call to step away from his profession and dedicate his life fully to the Gospel of Jesus Christ. Inspired by the divine mandate to *"…bring the healing Word and touch a dying world"* (Matthew 10:7-8), he has devoted his life to sharing God's truth and love with people from all walks of life. As a Cultural Architect, Conference Speaker, and Leadership & Change Consultant, Henry is a highly sought-after speaker for conferences and evangelistic crusades. He has ministered across the USA, Europe, and numerous cities in Africa, leading impactful outdoor Gospel campaigns. Wherever he goes, he carries the glory and power of God, offering transformative insights into Scripture that inspire believers to live faithfully, thrive spiritually, and prepare for Christ's return.

Serving as the Minister of Mountsorrel Baptist Church in Loughborough, UK, Henry wholeheartedly embraces his calling as a "reverse missionary," bringing the hope of the Gospel to communities across the United Kingdom. In addition, he leads as the president of Spirit Wind World Impact (SWWI), a mission-driven commission and foundation committed to spreading the healing Word of God and transforming lives through Gospel, educational, and medical outreach initiatives mainly in Africa. He is also a prolific author, having written more than 10 captivating inspirational titles.

Outside of his ministry, Henry enjoys football, writing, exploring nature, and spending precious time with his wife, Anita, and their children. His life and ministry stand as a testament to God's faithfulness and transforming power.

If you would like to receive further spiritual help or request any of our publications, please feel free to reach out to us at **henryohakah@icloud.com**, or visit our various social media handles:

- **X** (formerly Twitter): @doccharismata

- **TikTok:** @doccharismata

- **Instagram:** @doccharismata

- **YouTube:** @spiritwindwithhenry

- **Facebook:** @henrycohakah

To support you on your spiritual journey, we offer a collection of books and materials authored by Henry. These include:

1. The Attributes of God

2. Disturb Us, Lord: Musings of a "Reverse" Missionary

3. The I AM Sayings of Jesus Christ: An Evangelical Perspective

4. Come, Holy Spirit

5. Pregnant with Purpose

6. Be Yourself During Change: Preserving Self-Identity Through Life's Shifts

7. Tears in a Bottle

8. Retake Your Safe Space: The Art of Self-Encouragement

9. There is Gold in You: There's Something Inside of You Waiting to Get Out

10. Cultivating an Awareness of God's Presence: Nurturing Spiritual Intimacy

11. Footsteps of Giants

12. Rising in Faith: The Essential Handbook for Ministry

13. Speak to Your Future: You Are the Prophet of Your Own Life.

Spirit Wind World Impact

CONTACT INFORMATION:

EUROPE

Spirit Wind World Impact
UNITED KINGDOM
Email: henryohakah@icloud.com
Website: henryohakah.wixsite.com/swwi
YouTube: Spirit Wind with Henry

AFRICA

Henry Ohakah Foundation
54 Cameroun Road
PO Box 2721 UMUAHIA
NIGERIA
Phone: +234-802-451-1616
Email: henryohakah@gmail.com

Printed in Great Britain
by Amazon

60524282R00078

Do you love contemporary romance?

Want the chance to hear news about your favourite
authors (and the chance to win free books)?

Kristen Ashley
Ashley Herring Blake
Meg Cabot
Olivia Dade
Rosie Danan
J. Daniels
Farah Heron
Talia Hibbert
Sarah Hogle
Helena Hunting
Abby Jimenez
Elle Kennedy
Christina Lauren
Alisha Rai
Sally Thorne
Lacie Waldon
Denise Williams
Meryl Wilsner
Samantha Young

Then visit the Piatkus website
www.yourswithlove.co.uk

And follow us on Facebook and Instagram
www.facebook.com/yourswithlovex | @yourswithlovex

PIATKUS